Perspective!

This book is dedicated to educators for their passion and commitment in education. I am thankful for your contribution to our children's growth and development.

Perspective!

The Secret to Student Motivation and Success

Dr. Tommie Mabry

FOR INFORMATION:

Corwin

A SAGE Company

2455 Teller Road

Thousand Oaks, California 91320

(800) 233-9936

www.corwin.com

SAGE Publications Ltd.

1 Oliver's Yard

55 City Road

London EC1Y 1SP

United Kingdom

SAGE Publications India Pvt. Ltd.

B 1/I 1 Mohan Cooperative Industrial Area

Mathura Road, New Delhi 110 044

India

SAGE Publications Asia-Pacific Pte. Ltd.

18 Cross Street #10-10/11/12

China Square Central

Singapore 048423

President: Mike Soules

Vice President and Editorial Director: Monica Eckman

Program Director and Publisher: Dan Alpert

Senior Content Development Editor: Lucas Schleicher

Content Development Editor: Mia Rodriguez

Editorial Assistant: Natalie A. Delpino

Project Editor: Amy Schroller

Copy Editor: Shannon Kelly

Typesetter: Hurix Digital

Proofreader: Dennis Webb

Cover Designer: Rose Storey

Marketing Manager: Melissa Duclos

Printed in the United States of America

ISBN 978-1-0718-5615-4

This book is printed on acid-free paper.

22 23 24 25 26 10 9 8 7 6 5 4

Contents

PUBLISHER'S ACKNOWLEDGMENTS   vii

ABOUT THE AUTHOR   ix

INTRODUCTION   1

PROLOGUE   3

1 SHUT UP AND LISTEN...ACTIVELY: VALUE THE VOICES OF OTHERS   7

2 *SHOULD* IS A FUTILE WORD: BUILD YOUR STUDENTS UP WITH PRINCIPLES   17

3 RE-EXAMINE YOURSELF: DIG DEEP AND GO BEYOND BIASES   **26**

4 KNOW THEIR STRENGTHS: DEVELOP POSITIVE ATTITUDES AND STUDENT GROWTH   **35**

5 PUT YOURSELF IN THEIR SHOES: UNDERSTAND AND RESPOND TO THEIR WHYS   43

6 SHOW THEM YOU CARE: CREATE SAFE SPACES AND BUILD TRUST   51

7 GET THEM MOVING: ENGAGE THEM WITH KINESTHETIC AND COLLABORATIVE LEARNING   60

8 YOUR STUDENTS WILL TEACH YOU: CONNECT WITH CULTURALLY RESPONSIVE TEACHING   68

9 DREAMS LEAD TO EDUCATION: CAPTURE THEIR PASSIONS IN YOUR LESSONS   77

10 WHAT SHAPED MY PERSPECTIVE? YOUR STUDENTS NEED YOU   86

REFERENCES   93

INDEX   95

Publisher's Acknowledgments

Corwin gratefully acknowledges the contributions of the following reviewers:

Scott Bailey
Department Chair, Leadership and Administration
American College of Education
Indianapolis, IN

Ursula Y. Harris
Interventionist
Jackson Public Schools
Jackson, MS

Charles L. Lowery
Associate Professor of Educational Studies
Ohio University
Athens, OH

Nina Orellana
MTSS/Student Services Coordinator
Palm Bay Academy Charter School
Palm Bay, FL

About the Author

Dr. Tommie Mabry grew up in Jackson, Mississippi. Due to a lack of positive role models, Dr. Mabry turned to life in the streets. He was expelled from numerous schools, and by age eleven had been arrested for breaking and entering. Things started to change for Dr. Mabry when he joined an AAU basketball team that traveled around the world. Although he was shot in the foot  during his senior year, he received a full basketball scholarship to Missouri State University-West Plains. After completing his undergraduate studies at Tougaloo College, he taught school in the same district where he had been expelled numerous times. Subsequently, Dr. Mabry served as director of enrollment at Tougaloo College before founding the company that bears his name. He earned his PhD from Jackson State University and has published three books, *A Dark Journey to a Light Future*, *If Tommie Can Do It, We Can Do It*, and *Little Tommie's Four B's*.

Dr. Mabry's platform tackles the experiences and challenges that students face in communities and educational environments. By focusing on real-life topics such as bullying, life skills, classroom management, and more, he seeks to give students a positive outlook on teaching and learning and the ability to balance education and their lived experiences.

As an advocate for education and student success, Dr. Mabry travels around the country encouraging educators to focus on the whole student and motivating youth to never give up on hope.

Introduction

I've had the opportunity to travel to hundreds of schools across the country conducting professional development sessions with educators, assemblies with students, and small workshops with students who have been labeled "challenging" or "at risk."

Whenever possible, I try to publicly survey students on their perspectives during a live assembly with administrators and faculty present as witnesses. I begin by asking the students the following: "Raise your hand, and be honest, how many of you quickly bubble in answers on tests just to get done?" Inevitably, many hands go up. I then ask, "How many of you really don't like school?" Many hands go up again, and it's almost always the same students' hands. The difference between the students who are excelling and those who are not is now visible. I call this the *perspective gap*. I want to believe that most educators know that such a gap between achievers and nonachievers is not based on ability; in fact, some of the students with raised hands are quite brilliant.

In the course of responding to my first question, the students make it clear that this is not about ability but about the effort they put into the test. A common mantra among educators is "That student isn't dumb, they're just not trying." And this is usually spot-on. The students' lack of effort is simply a function of perspective and attitude, as evidenced by their responses to my second question during the assembly.

A critical point to keep in mind is that, like our brains, our perspectives can evolve and broaden. For this reason we must continue to teach to high expectations and adhere to the belief that even our most reticent students *can* learn, provided that they have a positive perspective on education. Still not convinced? How can I persuade you that even your hardest-to-reach students have the ability to learn? If you really want to see some of the world's smartest individuals, I suggest that you visit the correctional facilities around the world. I'm not being facetious. The ingenuity of incarcerated young men and women, who can accomplish amazing things with limited resources, never ceases to amaze me. I remember speaking to a young man in jail who painted my portrait using colored ink he made from scratch. You read that correctly: homemade colored ink. He told me that prior to his incarceration, he had never felt that he had a place in school, and he never saw himself doing any better than his parents. As our conversation came to a close, he told me, "My perspective toward school and life has changed since I've been locked up." Again, the key word here is *perspective*. What came out of his mouth next brought tears to my eyes: "If I could go back, I would take school seriously, because it's not like I didn't have the ability to do my work, I just couldn't see how $y=mx+b$ could change how my family was living."

Educators, if nothing else, this is my primary motivation for having written this book. How could we have intercepted this talented young man from embarking on the cradle-to-prison pipeline? (Delale-O'Connor et al. 2018). I could sense that, at his core, this was a good kid with the wrong perspective. I asked myself: *If he were my student, how could I have made school fun for him, how could I have taught him in a way that would have reached him, and how could I have exposed him to something that would have changed his outlook on school?* These are questions we must ask if we want to change a student's perspective.

Prologue

The first step to changing a child's perspective is to understand it.

Perspective: The Secret to Student Motivation and Success examines how to provide a space for students to develop a positive perspective on their formal education. It provides teachers with real-world insight into how shifting their own perspective on their students can transform the educational process. By taking a deep dive into what shapes students' perspectives, educators can better understand the beliefs, values, and experiences of students who have been labeled as "troubled" or "at risk." The strategies and underlying assumptions of this book are based not only on education research but on my own lived experience as well.

You see, I too was once labeled "at risk."

Any of us who have taught (or have raised children of our own) understand that every child is different. When teachers have a better understanding of their own perspectives, they can hone

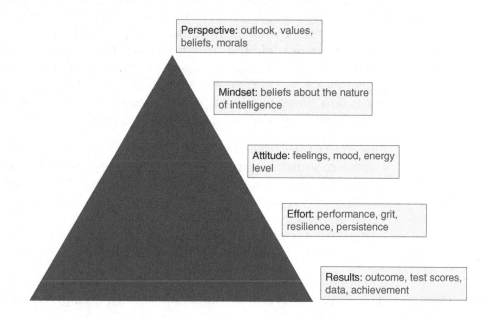

Perspective: outlook, values, beliefs, morals

Mindset: beliefs about the nature of intelligence

Attitude: feelings, mood, energy level

Effort: performance, grit, resilience, persistence

Results: outcome, test scores, data, achievement

their understanding of what shapes the student's perspective on school and act in a manner that expands the student's perspective.

This book offers insight on how *perspective determines effort*, meaning that the way a person views the impact or value of what that person does will always determine how that person acts or performs. When you approach an endeavor with a high level of integrity, a high level of excellence, and a high level of commitment, the outcome is likely to be positive. It's the effort that is put into something that yields results. By extension, such effort is often the difference between students who excel and those who don't.

⬅️➡️ PERSPECTIVE IS AT THE TOP OF THIS PYRAMID

Perspective is a holistic concept. A student's or teacher's perspective is influenced by a variety of factors including life experiences, cultural and environmental influences, how one is treated, and how one experiences the educational system as well as other institutions in the community. Perspective is positioned at the top of the pyramid because it informs mindset, attitudes, effort, and, ultimately, outcomes.

A *mindset* (Dweck 2007) refers to beliefs about the nature of intelligence. Students (and teachers) with a *fixed mindset* believe that intellectual ability is innate—i.e., you're either "born smart" or not. In contrast, a *growth mindset*, a concept that is supported by neuroscientific research, is based on the idea that intelligence is malleable—i.e., the brain can be grown like a muscle. It's easy to see how the overarching influence of perspective and one's mindset can result in the formation of positive or negative attitudes about school and, ultimately, the amount of effort that a student (or a teacher) exerts. And of course all of these influences flow down to results or outcomes such as assignments, student participation, and other measures of achievement.

Results are the consequences of your effort. It's the effort that is put into something that yields results. A key principle of this book is that achievement disparities are, among other things, a function of perspective. In order for teachers to bridge or close these disparities, they too must have the right perspective to understand their students. Similarly, a shift in student perspective that fuels increased effort can help reduce disparities.

This book offers strategies for expanding teachers' and students' perspectives, but, most importantly, it emphasizes the need to better understand our students and the influences on their perspectives that begin early in life.

...

Feelings and thoughts can change by the second. Achievement doesn't occur in a vacuum and emotions play a key role. When we feel that our safety is under threat, our ability to learn is deeply compromised (Hammond 2015). Since we are controlled by our moods, if a student and teacher are both in a good mood on a particular day, both are likely to put effort into their respective teaching and learning. The corollary is that if the mood of one of them changes, so changes the effort. Moods may be powerful, but attempting to shift or regulate moment-by-moment feelings is, at best, a band-aid. Changing one's perspective—the holistic concept that encompasses mindsets, attitudes, emotions, and, ultimately, one's effort—amounts to a long-term change. Changing a person's perspective is a deeper-level endeavor in that it cuts to the core of that person's beliefs and values, all of which are shaped by that person's life experiences.

For example, if a school community is preparing for a state test, the principal might plan a morale-building event for the students and staff. Such "pep rallies" may result in a temporary uptick in morale around test taking and might even motivate some students to put more effort into taking the test. However, such a surface-level event is no guarantee that the students' perspective towards school will change.

I'll also offer a personal example of the relationship between fleeting emotions and deeper-level perspectives. My daughter is in the second grade, and her class uses a color system to denote the students' moods throughout the day. When she comes home with a certain color that is satisfying, she is in a great mood. And that mood is further sustained after my wife and I remind her that she is a good student and that it is important for her to follow directions in class. She usually goes back to school the next day with a positive attitude. However, over the course of a few days, she might revert to being a color that is not as pleasing—a reflection of her mood change. In her case, her mindset ("I can do this!") and attitude ("I love this!") can vary according to her mood. A positive mood and attitude alone aren't strong enough to change her behavior as a whole. Her behavior is unlikely to change until her perspective (the overarching concept) has shifted.

When your perspective shifts, the change is deep-seated and involves your outlook, viewpoints, values, beliefs, and even morals. Like my daughter, until you make such a holistic change, in all likelihood you will continue to revert to normal behaviors. More specifically, if your perspective is that school isn't for you, then you will believe that sitting in a school building is a waste of time. To sum up:

> **Attitude** reflects a feeling—e.g., the way I feel about school.

> **Mindset** is a set of beliefs around my (or others') intellectual capacity.

> **Perspective** is a holistic view based on a variety of factors. It can be grounded in a number of beliefs and values, including the belief that there are more important (or more valuable) ways to spend my time than in school.

Your perspective determines your thoughts, and your thoughts create a chain reaction that leads to taking actions that make you feel either good or bad about yourself and your life. One's perspective can predetermine the outcome. Perspective is the lens through which we see the world and that determines how we approach everything around us and interact with other people.

Let's be honest: Enrichment programs and other resources can help fuel motivation and achievement, but if a student's negative perspective of school remains fixed, the research suggests the consequences are negative academic outcomes, including increased likelihood of dropping out. Even if we can convince our students to show up, their perspectives will determine their levels of effort. You may not know it, but as an educator you can exert tremendous influence over your students' perspectives. That is the overarching theme of this book.

CHAPTER 1

Shut Up and Listen…Actively

Value the Voices of Others

The simple act of listening could shape your perspective on teaching. You, as an educator, person, parent, friend, sibling, etc., already have your own perspective, which likely won't change very much if you keep talking. Stephen King, American author and guru of science fiction and horror genres, once said that

> the important question has nothing to do with whether the talk in your story is sacred or profane; the only question is how it rings on the page and in your ear. If you expect it to ring true, then you must talk yourself. Even more important, you must *shut up and listen* to others talk.

Stephen King's net worth is over nine figures, and most of us would agree that he is quite successful. He did not reach such a pinnacle by just telling others what he thought was important; rather, he was quiet at times and listened to the voices and needs of others. This rings true with even some of the most mundane types of human interaction. I know there have been many times in my life where in order for me to reach a level of self-understanding I had to listen rather than just be heard. But what about someone in a position of authority?

LISTENING IS NOT JUST HEARING

How many times have you wanted to get your point across so badly that you found yourself talking over the other person? What mattered most to you was to be heard—not understood or valued—but *heard*. Imagine being in a place where you cannot voice your opinion; instead, you must sit and take what someone forces on you with no argument. You are imagining a traditional classroom. In such classrooms children must sit and take what is doled out to them as the gospel truth, speak only when asked a question, speak only at a certain volume, direct their words to a particular audience, and make the words' subjects and verbs agree—rules that never seem to allow much wiggle room for natural communication. Your students crave the opportunity to be heard, even in your classroom.

Children's Healthcare of Atlanta is a nonprofit philanthropic organization geared toward providing outreach and healthcare services to urban families in the metro Atlanta area. Based in an area with a great need for persons seeking to address social disparities, this nonprofit group has pioneered a concerted effort to give parents and educators insight on kids' most basic requirements. According to the organization's website, it offers valuable insight on a child's need to be heard and what results when a child does not feel heard:

> There's no question that the middle school and high school years are tough. Social challenges follow kids home on their phones; academic pressure can be intense; and scary issues such as gun violence are all over the news. You might talk with your child about their feelings—but are you really listening?
>
> You may be surprised to know that a lot of middle schoolers don't confide in their parents—and they don't think their parents are listening when they do. One middle schooler in a Children's Healthcare of Atlanta focus group wished their parents would start "listening to my thoughts and feelings instead of interrupting and saying it's not that big of a deal." Another said, "I want them to listen to what I'm saying, not just tell me to suck it up and say 'you're fine.'"

When *our* perspective prevents us from shutting up and listening, we don't allow a child to open up verbally, emotionally, and cognitively. Children can sense when an adult shows up with a closed mind. In response, they won't openly share what they want to say, and nothing can enter their minds either. A barrier in communication can impede any potential for learning. Consequently, your perspective as an educator, including being willing to open up to what a student has to say to you, can make all the difference.

I remember working at one of the most impoverished middle schools in my state. I decided to compare notes with a colleague who worked at one of the most disadvantaged high schools in the same state. He lamented that his school had the highest of everything negative and the lowest of everything positive. Highest drop out rate? Had it. Highest teen pregnancy rate? Had it. Highest retention rate? Had it. Highest number of overaged and undercredited students? Had it. Worst of all, they had the lowest graduation rate. Imagine being in a classroom where you are already labeled as "at risk" and have no say in what or how you are being taught. Listening to my colleague relate the conditions at his high school is when I realized that the young people in my middle school deserved to be heard. So I shut up and listened.

Silence is the language of God, all else is poor translation. — **Rumi**

Rumi, who is often referred to as the greatest mystical poet in the world, had a great understanding of connectedness. He spoke of not just a connection to God, but how we as people make a connection with others by having our own understanding of self and how we are connected by even the most practical things. He spoke of how we connect to the universe by connecting with the words and thoughts of others. He is well known for detailing some of the smallest of interactions with grace and respect. This general respect for living is seen in his poems and other works. The joyous love sonnets this Persian writer and spiritualist brought into the world over eight centuries ago are still held dear by a large number of educators and academicians alike. Rumi is frequently portrayed as a forward thinker, and his sonnets have been beloved readings at weddings and funerals for many years. Why? Because his knowledge of extending love is seen as most fitting at weddings and funerals—places where people are revered, doted upon, and, most importantly, loved.

Most Americans appreciate the need to be quiet at weddings and funerals because the attendees are encouraged to reflect and, at times, even genuflect. Now ask yourself why such a degree of respect and attentiveness is rarely directed at the children who inhabit our classrooms? Particularly when working to educate children who may not see school as a loving space, one must be quiet to find out how these students feel. Listen to what students have to say; get their perspective on education and the world around them. When I permitted myself to listen, I was stunned to discover that students I worked with who had been labeled as "at risk" or "unreachable"—or, even worse, "stupid"— actually were extremely thoughtful, savvy, and loving. They had just never had anyone take the time to shut up and listen to *them* rather than forcing opinions on them. Once I permitted myself to shut up and listen, I was able to value my students for just coming to class. During a professional development workshop I gave at a high school, I ran into a colleague who wanted to share an intriguing story about the powerful insights she had gained from listening to one of her students:

> I had one student, a single mother of two in the twelfth grade. She missed a lot of class, frequently fell asleep, and was on her phone quite a bit. I became frustrated when I asked her to repeat something that seemed so small to me from the textbook and was faced with her looking up at me like a deer in headlights. I then asked her to step outside the class with me as I launched the rest of the class into their lesson. I didn't have to say anything; I just listened. I knew she was a teen mom, but it was at that moment that she began to tell me stories of how her oldest child suffered from a rare disorder that kept him up at night; thus, she was up with him. His medication was quite expensive, and she worked two part-time jobs to afford it. As soon as she left school each day at 1:00 p.m., she went straight to work until 8:00 p.m., got her children from her grandmother's house, and stayed with them until they fell asleep around 10:00 p.m. She then would leave them with her younger sister at home because her mother also worked nights. She clocked in at her night job at a fast food restaurant at 11:00 p.m. and worked there until 4:00 a.m. She had just enough time to go back home, shower, and sleep a few hours before she did it all over again. This young lady was a survivor, and once I listened I valued her presence even more. She knew her education was important, and she was determined to graduate no matter what. And she did, with honors. Once I shut up and listened, I no longer let my frustration about a lesson get in the way of the truer and deeper connection that I was beginning to develop with my students.

⬅ LIKE MOMMA USED TO SAY, "CLOSE YOUR MOUTH AND OPEN YOUR EARS."

Researchers discuss the benefit of what is called *active listening*, which is a skill that puts the onus on you as the recipient of a message in a conversation. When practicing active listening, the recipient of a message is quiet and takes time to take in what the other person is saying. Active listening is a skill that can be perfected through many methods, and in the case of educators, active listening allows the person speaking to clearly communicate his or her message to the recipient in order for a conversation to grow deeper, into a realm of understanding.

BECOME AN ACTIVE LISTENER

In the 2007 article "Learning to Listen: Teaching an Active Listening Strategy to Preservice Education Professionals," the authors delve into how the skill of listening allows persons to come across as being more trustworthy. The authors state that

> the goal in active listening is to develop a clear understanding of the speaker's concern and also to **clearly communicate the listener's interest in the speaker's message**. Recognition of the importance of active listening has resulted in systematic investigation of the use of active listening skills in other helping professions. In a study examining the communication skills of nurses as they worked with families experiencing a medical emergency, Duhamel and Talbot (2004) reported that the use of active listening skills helped nurses to establish a trusting relationship with family participants. Mansfield (1991) used supervised roleplays to teach active listening skills to medical students; based on a videotape analysis of their pre- and post-instruction performances, the medical students who had received training were judged to be more skilled in their use of active listening skills and in developing appropriate management plans for their patients. (p. 224)

Bedside manner is used in hospitals to soothe nervous or frantic patients. The key trait the participants in the Mansfield study displayed was an ability to show the patient with whom they were speaking that the patient's message was valid and, most of all, valuable. The study also elaborated on how, by practicing active listening, these participants earned more respect from their patients than medical professionals who had double the experience in the field. They were able to build trust and also make a connection just through active listening. Now let's equate that to teaching.

As educators, if you shut up and listen to your students, not only will you learn something and gain a new perspective but you will be able to build your relationship with the student at the same time. This is why it's important to listen. In the Mansfield study, the medical students found success with their patients and in their field by showing how much they cared, and that began with listening. They were able to build trust with their patients, and through this trust they were able to make a lasting impression. It takes asking the right questions to make such a connection.

➡ MAKE A CONNECTION BY ASKING THE RIGHT QUESTIONS

The goal in the chapter is to allow you, the reader, to have a better appreciation for the art of silence and to get to know students with different experiences than you so you can begin to recognize and understand their perspectives. Once you are able to be quiet and listen, you must allow your curiosity to be piqued—although not in a nosy next-door neighbor type of way. Rather, you want to be seen as one who can be trusted by making an empathetic connection. In order to ask the right questions after you have listened, try to put yourself in the student's shoes and look at their world through their perspective. You do not have to come from the same part of town to make a connection; with a little probing, you most certainly can make a connection with students that have even the most disparate backgrounds and interests.

Making a connection by asking questions about a student's food and music preferences can be a great icebreaker, but asking questions such as "How do you feel today?" "Did you eat breakfast?" "How's your family doing?" or "What makes you most excited about the upcoming school year?" can make a connection that is deeper and more substantial.

➡ HOW CAN YOU FULLY TEACH SOMEBODY YOU DON'T KNOW?

In the situation mentioned earlier involving my colleague and her student who was a single teen mother of two, it might seem that the two women probably did not have much in common. However, once my colleague was able to be quiet and listen to her student, she asked the one question that allowed them to connect: "What do you need from me to make you the most successful?" Not only was the student taken aback by that, she felt that her teacher genuinely cared for her, her children, and her mental well-being—not just her grades. My colleague was able to connect with her even more by sharing a time in school when she did not have a teacher who was able to allow her to just exist without feeling singled out. She also told her student that she could empathize with working two jobs. Even though she did not have to do that as a teen parent, my colleague knew how hard it was for her as an adult, and she told her student she would assist in making accommodations to assignments when possible. The empathy and vulnerability that was expressed allowed them to make a genuine connection, and my colleague was able to see her student thrive instead of just survive.

 ## USE YOUR SERVICE-MINDEDNESS TO HELP SHAPE YOUR PERSPECTIVE

As most of us know, teaching is a service, and in the article "Improving Classroom Management Issues by Building Connections with Families" (Robison 2020), the author details how making yourself vulnerable will allow you to make a deeper connection with your students:

> Coming from a place of service is a mind-set that will guide one's words and actions. In short, it is to simply realize that a general...teacher's job is to serve all students and their families, much like other public servants or even members of the clergy. As...teachers, we are unique in our role of serving all students, not just those that self-select into performing....While there are limitations to this mind-set, such as setting reasonable boundaries for your time and not catering to every whim of every family, coming from a place of service can help in communicating potentially tense issues with family members. (p. 39)

Applying such a service mindset needn't be restricted to your interactions with family members. It can also work in the interest of making an empathetic connection with your students—a connection that can offer more success than you can imagine. There is one proviso, however: You have to be open enough to shut up and listen to them. When you are curious about a student's world and ask questions to understand things, you are automatically expanding both your perspective and your horizons. Take this time to access both your own and the student's perspective so you can come up with innovative ways to shift both.

HOW TO LISTEN

Active listening requires patience and practice, but those who take the time to engage in it will strengthen their connections with students in powerful ways. Moreover, if we strengthen these relationships with cultural awareness and relevance (a subject that is explored in more depth later in this book), our connections will be even stronger. For now, there are two general principles to keep in mind:

- Learn the culture of the student's community where you work.

- Center your efforts around gaining a perspective that is conducive for reaching all students, beginning with a reflection on your own biases.

CHECK YOUR BIASES AT THE DOOR

A prerequisite to shutting up and listening is checking your own biases and prejudgments at the door. For example, when you begin to engage in a conversation with a student, stop thinking about how you think the conversation will go. Even if you have tried to engage with this student before on many other occasions, you must not prejudge how you think the conversation is going to go *this* time. Since you are now approaching the conversation with new knowledge, insights, and clarity, you should clear everything from past interactions out of your mind.

CHECK YOUR BODY LANGUAGE

Body language can tell a person everything. And in many cases, *uncaring* body language will make recipients shut down because they believe you have already formulated an outcome before an interaction has even happened. Believe it or not, our body language can change an entire conversation before it has begun. Reflect on your own interpersonal interactions: What is the message you receive from folded arms and a head cocked to the side? Refrain from any body language that shows you are not interested because your student will instantly become defensive and not open up. Part of shutting up and listening is learning to relax.

CHECK AND RELEASE PAST INTERACTIONS

You may miss an opportunity to really connect with your students when they are opening up and allowing themselves to vent if you are sitting on the sidelines and anxiously waiting for a specific outcome. You will be pleasantly surprised when, instead of forming judgments based on past experiences, you use this time to relax your mind and body language to be open to what the students has to tell you. Sadly enough, you do not know it all, especially when it comes to the hearts, minds, and experiences of students. For this reason, particularly in the early stages of engaging with your students, open *your* heart and mind!

Dos and Don'ts

We close each chapter with a summary list of Dos and Don'ts, followed by a reflection. Use this space and time to prepare yourself as you begin this new journey as an educator with a more enlightened perspective.

DO:

- Present your body language in a relaxed and open stance.

- Make eye contact with your students as they are talking.

- Give students adequate space to feel comfortable, but be close enough for them to know you are engaging in a conversation (approximately two to three feet apart).

- Respond using a caring voice, being careful to avoid inflections on words that may be perceived as accusatory.

- Have an open mind in response to what your students have to say.

- Listen from a place of understanding.

- Allow your students to be heard without judgment.

- Close your mouth more and open your ears.

DON'T:

- Form an answer in your head—i.e., form your own hypothesis—before you get a response. This not only works against active listening but leads to judging the student before hearing what the student has to say.

- Make facial expressions that can unconsciously express a bias.

- Use or make gestures while your student is talking—for example, no hands thrown in the air, hands on your hips, or any sarcastic gesture that will make a child shut down.

- Assume the negative immediately.

- Force your opinion of learning on your student.

- Overtalk your student for the sake of exerting your authority.

- Go another day without reflecting on how you have affected others by not being responsive to what they are saying.

Chapter Reflection

This chapter has emphasized the importance of silence and also the benefit that comes from active listening. The end of each chapter offers a space for work and reflection. Workshops can be very useful and inspiring, but in the absence of teacher reflection, they are unlikely to have much influence on improving your craft. Now is the time for us to think and to write.

Think and write about a time when you made a connection with a student that was meaningful. Think and reflect on what made that connection meaningful and also what could have made it even more significant.

_____

_____

_____

_____

Think of a time when you missed an opportunity to connect with a student through active listening. Did you spend too much time talking when you could have been quiet? What questions could you have asked that student?

_____

_____

_____

_____

How do you think you can make a connection with a student in the future? Take the time to plan a specific time to make this connection and think deeply about your response.

_____

_____

_____

_____

CHAPTER 2

Should Is a Futile Word

Build Your Students up With Principles

When I was younger, I hated being told what I *should* do. I now realize that my aversion was a response to the feeling that I was being relegated into submission. That feeling never really goes away, even as an adult. I recently experienced it while in conversation with a friend about something as mundane as replacing the tires on my car. I had already scheduled an appointment with a nationally recognized and reputable auto service establishment, but when I mentioned this to my friend, he took it upon himself to tell me, "You *should* take it to my cousin; he can save you a lot of money." That one word—*should*— instantly put me in a different headspace. I no longer felt that I was having an equal conversation with my peer; rather, it felt like I was being scolded. I was made to feel that my choice was not valid, although taking my car to his cousin had not even been an option until he brought it up in the moment.

Part of being human is that we sometimes find ourselves in positions where our natural inclination is to fight or flee. When things get tough or scary, or we feel backed into a corner, we become argumentative or we abandon the situation altogether. In this case, when I was told what I *should* do after I had done my research and felt comfortable with my own decision, my fight or flight response was to grow defensive.

In this case the word *should* was my trigger. Even if my friend had good intentions (and I assume he did), his language had a very different impact on me. I read it an attempt *to force me into a decision by being judgmental.*

Even if we think we know better than our students, when you impose your own view of what others *should* do upon them, expect to be disappointed. Oftentimes, the limitations of our own perspectives result in false assumptions about our students and, in the worst case, we create self-fulfilling prophecies of predictable failure. In this chapter we take a close look at how the disparities between educator and student perspectives can have unintended, even devastating consequences.

Most educators have been exposed to the ideas of Charles Darwin. Darwin's premise that *only the strong survive* is just part of the story. The second part is *adaptation*—the idea that, in order to survive, species must adapt (or evolve) in response to changes in their environment.

People, according to Darwin, are no different. We adapt or we perish depending upon whether or not we are able to adapt to change. But let's face it, *change is hard*. And what about unpredictable and sudden changes to our environment, such as floods, famines, and hurricanes? When we encounter such sudden outliers, we either quickly adapt—e.g., flee our immediate surroundings—or fight it out in the hopes of surviving. This metaphor can also be applied to our students. When students feel like they are being backed into a corner and bombarded with messages that they *should* act in a way that is different from how they have always acted in order to survive, a fair amount of dissonance is inevitable.

SURVIVAL OF THE FITTEST

I grew up in a family where merely surviving took precedence over formal education. I have vivid memories of the messaging from my early childhood: *Get a job to help support my family as well as myself.* I was never told that education was a key to a better life. The perspective I grew up with was one that prioritized landing a job and earning a living. In fact, there was no other choice in life for people like me. Our survival depended upon making money, and the relationship between formal education and earning good wages was never acknowledged. This perspective simply didn't jive with the messaging that I later received in school, all of which focused on the actions I *should* take to become a better student. Again, I could see no connection between spending hours in a classroom and making sufficient income to survive. There was no way for me to conceptualize a payoff ten or twelve years down the road when I needed to eat *now*. However, like most things in life, my school experience was nuanced. There were times that I did tune into school and even completed some assignments. Yet I didn't apply myself to what I was told I *should* be doing to succeed in school. To extend the Darwinian metaphor, in a world in which only the "fittest" survive, school was not part of what made me "fit" to survive my family or my neighborhood. Only later, when I finally felt I was being heard, was I able to change my perspective.

I have a clear childhood memory of being asked to complete a math assignment in school. Initially, I did not understand the assignment, and before I knew it, my teacher said out loud, "You should know this; we went over it yesterday." Her meaning was clear: She was making light of the fact that I had not been in school at all that week. But in fact there was nothing funny about her remark. She made no attempt to understand why I had not been in school the previous day (I had had a good reason to be absent). Because I had already been labeled as a problem, she wanted to further demoralize me with yet another *should*—in this case, what I *should* already know. Of course, the absurd expectation that I should be familiar with this new content only existed in the teacher's mind, not mine. So, predictably enough, I shut down completely. I relive this painful story only to reinforce why I believe *should* is a potentially harmful word that we should banish from our vocabulary.

Not only is this *should* type of thinking damaging to a child, it is also dangerous. I was not shown how; rather I was just told what I *should* be doing. But how could I know what to do when the *should* in question didn't fit my perspective, a perspective that was based on my need to survive? It did not even exist in my mind.

◀▶ SHOULD HASN'T EVEN HAPPENED YET

In the above example, my teacher openly compared me to other students. I now understand that just because other students clocked in more school hours than me did not make me less than them. I was trained to be a hustler, and comparing me to others who didn't need to struggle to survive created an unfair judgment. Most educators concur (at least in theory) that differentiating our teaching to meet a spectrum of diverse learning needs is a best practice. In contrast, the assumption that all students share a common perspective is misguided and leads to the assumption that the teacher's expectations (the *shoulds*) are shared by every student.

Let's look at some basic behavioral expectations: *This kid should walk in a straight line. This kid should not sleep in class.* Although such expectations are commonly held, have you ever thought about why that one child is impulsive and has difficulty walking in a straight line? Or about how another student juggles multiple jobs at night, making it difficult for her to stay awake? In such cases, even what we consider the most reasonable of expectations may place undue strain on the student in a manner that makes school feel like a correctional institution. For those of you who think this is far-fetched, consider the national data on the *cradle to prison pipeline* (Delale-O'Connor et al. 2018)—a system of oppression that has been with us for generations.

CHANGING YOUR BELIEF SYSTEM

I'll say it again: Banish the word *should* from your belief system. Basing behavior on common expectations for each child is unrealistic and damaging since every child grows up in different circumstances and holds a unique perspective. Those of us born into generational poverty where the fight for bare survival supersedes all other needs are driven by a different imperative than those with privilege. This doesn't mean that we lower our standards or push some children into remedial course work (another form of "imprisonment"). However, as stated previously, before we jump to impose our *shoulds* on our students, we must first shut up and listen, which builds the bridge to understanding where each child is coming from.

Should is a futile word. It's about what didn't happen. It belongs in a parallel universe. It belongs in another dimension of space. — **Margaret Atwood**

This quote, from the renowned Canadian writer Margaret Atwood, popular for her award-winning novels, short stories, and poetry, including the dystopian novel (now a TV series) *The Handmaid's Tale*, provides us with a unique perspective on why *should* is a word that has an expiration date, especially when we continually provide rules of engagement with students within a classroom.

Atwood mentions that *should* cannot be measured because it is an opinion. *Should* does not exist in objective reality; rather, it is just in the mind of the speaker. As Atwood alludes, *should* makes us become defensive and puts us on our guard. It also can make us feel inept or inferior when, in fact, the *should* only exists in the imagination of the accuser. The *shoulds* of school connote an imaginary "model student" and are often based on a set of imaginary rules.

⬅️ TEACHING PRINCIPLES RATHER THAN RULES

In school we learn that rules rule—a belief that is typically unquestioned. But, at their core, most rules are set for mere compliance and are a byproduct of *should* belief systems. As previously discussed, harping on the *should* can immediately place students in a glass box they can only escape by punching their way out (fighting) or by jumping out and leaving altogether (fleeing). Again, the mismatch between teacher and student perspectives sets false expectations for all parties involved.

In *Life Learning Magazine,* Robyn Coburn (2020) eloquently details how rules can set false expectations for children and can easily be shaped into principles:

> Rules are a two sided, oxymoronic coin—on one side the expectation of automatic compliance, on the other side the punishment for breakage. Rules for children are often not designed to be useful in themselves but function as molds, designed to teach some idea, especially the idea that rules must be followed, without defiance or even contemplation.

> These are the skills that they then bring into adult life. The few rules in a child's life that might be useful, such as "don't turn on the stove when Mommy is out," can be simply and easily converted into principles that can allow for empowered exploration and make real sense to a freely living child. These only reiterate how ineffective and inefficient arbitrary rule making (or expressing rules in a manner that makes them seem arbitrary) is in itself.

Coburn suggests that the *shoulds* are typically formed from rules that sustain oppression. A rule to walk on the right side of the hall holds less weight than that of a taught principle to avoid running into someone else and getting hurt. Teaching a child a principle to avoid harm allows them to have life skills rather than being bound by rules that may not match their conception of the real world. For example, instead of saying, "Be quiet in the line—stay in a straight line— don't get out of line in the hall," break down the principles of showing others around you respect and how to have empathy for other students' needs.

Also, explain how it could hinder other people's learning when there is too much noise in the hall, or how character is demonstrated when we move together as a unit to the lunch-room. Such examples of teachable moments depict how to positively influence a child rather than impose superficial rules without explanation.

➡️ PRINCIPLES HELP BUILD UP A CHILD

Coburn goes on to state that domestic life for many children is defined by petty, unaccommodating rules that treat them as dishonest or intrinsically deceitful. Because the adults in these households don't have to follow the same rules, children quickly perceive that such rules are meant to be "followed," and do not connect them with the principles upon which they are based. Principles, on the other hand, are meant for everyone in the household and extend into daily life at school and elsewhere. Children best learn principles like courtesy and kindness not when they are instructed to "be good," but when they see adults modeling that behavior.

You must admit that it's hard for us as adults to obey the rules we set, so just imagine how difficult it is for the students. For most adults it's hard to be quiet after sitting in silence for hours. Even for me, if I can't talk in the lunchroom while I'm eating, or in the hall as I pass my colleagues, when do I get to release? If you think about it, it is unnatural to be forced to pass your friend without speaking, so why force your students to do the same? Students shouldn't feel like they are sentenced to twelve years in school; school is not forced incarceration. However, the manner in which we enforce our arbitrary rules makes it seem that way.

One day I had a speaking engagement at a school in California where I noticed an unusual lunchtime scene. The kids were outside on their skateboards, listening to music, dancing, and lying on the lawn. It was more like a college setting than any K–12 school I had visited. I asked the principal, "Why do these kids have so much freedom and how do you keep them in line?" His response was, "That's the thing: We don't try to keep them in line, we teach them respect and we build a system that lets them be themselves and be under less pressure." I thought to myself, *Wow, this is what school can be!* When the kids were done socializing, they went back to class and continued to complete their work. No yelling, no violence, no issuing demerits, just a seamless transition. That's because the school as a whole worked; the adults had laid a solid foundation down that was enforced by principles.

The principal also told me that the students rarely fought outside, and I thought to myself, *This couldn't happen where I'm from.* But I then caught myself. I realized that I was articulating a mindset and a set of beliefs that something was impossible to achieve. When this becomes a cultural perspective, we limit our creativity due to the limitations of our own beliefs and imagination. I had to realign myself and see that there was nothing different between these students and the students I interacted with back home. The only thing that was different was their perspective.

I was also amazed that the staff wasn't outside. The principal told me that his teachers took their break together; that was their time to release also. "We teach our students that people shouldn't have to stand over them for them to act right," he said to me. At that point, I had an epiphany: That principle, based on agency and self-sufficiency, gave the kids freedom and also made them look forward to coming to school—it allowed them to have fun and not be threatened by the fear of breaking arbitrary rules.

The secret to changing our students' perspectives begins with changing the system that they inhabit. Substituting rules with principles is one example of such a change. As Coburn (2020) states, "Children who live surrounded by rules, instead of learning about principles, end up becoming adept at getting around rules, finding the loopholes in rules, disguising non-compliance or deflecting blame for non-compliance (i.e., lying about what they did)."

Dos and Don'ts

Ironically, our list of Dos and Don'ts may be reminiscent of the very rules we have critiqued in this chapter. However, their purpose is to remind educators that checking our *should* at the door will ultimately liberate our students from the incarceration of oppressive systems and allow them to become their best selves.

DO:

- Teach principles rather than rules.
- Build a child up through explaining the importance of principles.

- Hone your understanding of the damaging effects unrealistic expectations have on a child.

- Remove *should* from your vocabulary when talking with your students.

- Look at each student through a fresh lens and take that student's background and life experiences into consideration when communicating.

- Remember that many urban and marginalized students come from a place of survival and "doing school" does not mesh with such a perspective until you work to shift it.

DON'T:

- Relegate your students to what they *should* be doing.

- Create baseless rules for mere compliance.

- Compare students to each other in terms of ability.

- Assume you can ascertain a student's perspective with respect to what is important in that student's life.

- Assume that all students share your expectations.

Chapter Reflection

This chapter has explored the danger of *should* in our schools and classrooms. We can't possibly build connections with our students if we hold them to a predetermined paradigm that is likely at odds with their perspectives, particularly if those perspectives are built on their assumptions of what it takes to survive. Take the time to reflect on the questions below. Now is the time for us to think and to write.

Think and write about a time when you told a student what that student should be doing. How was that expectation received by the student?

_____

_____

_____

_____

Was there ever a time when you could have been more open to learning about a student's family or home life? Can you now see if that student was responding to you from a survival perspective?

_____

_____

_____

_____

Where in your lessons can you build in a time to gain insight into a student's home life and neighborhood to fully grasp if that student is responding from a survival perspective?

_____

_____

_____

_____

CHAPTER 3

Re-examine Yourself

Dig Deep and Go Beyond Biases

Today's students are different from their predecessors of even a few generations ago. Our parents and grandparents were shaped by numerous social inequities that skewed their perspectives. If you are a descendant of Black Americans, you most certainly have heard stories of enslaved generations, the Jim Crow era, and the struggle for civil rights. If you are a descendent of immigrant Americans, you most certainly have heard stories of the search for a better life, the Great Depression, and how these factors shaped your family's story. If you are a descendent of Jewish Americans, you most certainly have heard stories of the horrendous atrocities that befell your ancestors over the course of generations at the hands of evil dictators, the struggle to live and survive during times of hate and fear, and how these struggles shaped your past generations. Even though today's students are not directly affected by some of these struggles, their stories are just as richly shaped: Surviving a pandemic is just the most recent example of endurance in the face of pain and hardship.

Looking at the past must only be a means of understanding more clearly what and who they are so that they can more wisely build the future. — **Paulo Freire**

Paulo Freire's celebrated book, *Pedagogy of the Oppressed* (1972), looks critically at the importance of understanding a marginalized student's perspective when faced with a system that was designed to serve students and families of greater wealth, power, and influence. On its website, the Freire Institute describes his work as one encompassing education, community development, and community health. Freire always understood that education can be either passive or active: a matter of mere accumulation of knowledge or an engaging activity in which learners participate in the world around them. Critically, knowledge and action are closely linked. As the Freire Institute's website puts it, "it is essential that people link knowledge to action so that they actively work to change their societies at a local level and beyond." In education, one's society, like Mr. Freire mentions, is paramount, and once we as educators take that huge factor into consideration we can begin to dissect the layers that have hardened some of our most "difficult" students.

THE BLUE SUIT

What has remained a constant, however, through our ever-changing generations is that our interaction with students can be skewed by each other's lived experiences and, more often than not, implicit biases carried through generations. Recall the story in Chapter 1 about a teacher's experience with her student who was a teen mom. That teacher and I engaged in another conversation about perspective that concerned a discussion she had held with her students about joining an honors academy she had created at her school.

> I worked really hard with the principal at that time to create a space that I thought the kids would aspire to be a part of. I taught great kids, but I wanted them to also help me to motivate others to do better in school, so I worked with the principal to create honors classes that grew into an honors academy. I had worked with a few select teachers to offer a more rigorous curriculum to a cohort of twenty-five students. It was a lot of fun at first; they even told their friends and we grew to over forty kids within a month. These kids were not the not the most high performing by any means, but since we gave them more privileges they were willing to do more rigorous work and they saw it was not that bad. I even added more things to the program, like service projects, eating lunch in class or outside, and eventually we all wore matching navy blazers, white shirts, and navy bottoms—real business-like! Well, then I noticed more and more that my students stopped bringing their lunches back to the class, they stopped eating outside, and finally they began to slowly no longer wear their business suits. I had had enough, so I called a meeting with my cohort and asked them what was going on. We all sat in our meeting space (yes, I had gotten an old

storage classroom cleared out to become our meeting space/study hall) and we just talked. And through that conversation I realized that my honors students were receiving pushback from their friends in their neighborhood when they walked to school in their uniforms. They would get followed and even harassed as they walked to school. The people in their circle ostracized them. They were eventually ridiculed by their peers and made to feel like they were "sellouts." And anyone from an urban setting knows that one of the worst things a person can be is a sellout. I felt so bad because I thought that I was showing them fun stuff and allowing them to be an example to their peers, but that peer pressure was so strong that they could not stand being labeled as a "sellout" anymore. No one else in their neighborhood had parents or even grandparents who wore business suits every day. That suit was not seen as a badge of honor; rather, it was seen as the mark of a traitor. So my student's peers made them victims of their own biases of how someone who was a sellout or a snitch looked: dressed in a navy blue suit.

My colleague learned a valuable lesson in regard to perspective. What she thought was a good and positive influence actually backfired, and her kids were left feeling like outcasts rather than pillars of their community. Even though the honors academy was a great influence on her students, my colleague wasn't clued in to the potential backlash that her students would receive from their peers. Her perspective, formed by her own lived experiences, led her to believe that participating in an honors class was a great distinction that others aspired to. It was only when she allowed space to listen to her students that she understood the disconnect between her perspective and that of many of the residents in the students' neighborhood. To these residents the blue suit signified the mark of a traitor and was therefore an impediment to her students' well-being and survival.

COLONIZERS

Paulo Freire underscored a concept that provides insight on this example of "traitor" thinking. In *Pedagogy of the Oppressed*, he explains the concept of the colonized versus the colonizers. The idea is straightforward: When outsiders (the colonizers) enter a community in which they haven't been raised or acculturated, they tend to impose their way of life or thinking on the people within that community (the colonized), even if unknowingly.

Freire stated that "those who authentically commit themselves to the people must re-examine themselves constantly" (Heick n.d.) As an educator coming into an outside community, my colleague failed to realize what those blue suits represented.

To the students, the blue suits were a symbol of oppression. Lawyers who put their family members in jail through misrepresentation wore blue suits. The landlords who neglected to upkeep their apartment buildings wore blue suits. And, even worse, the police that plagued and profiled them and had been doing so for generations wore blue (albeit differently tailored) suits. My colleague did not make that connection at the time; she thought the suits looked "professional," but her difference in perspective, compounded by not having engaged in the kind of self-examination that Freire insists upon, set her up for failure.

However, this updated knowledge of how the suits were perceived (as well as the perception that students selected to be in this program received special treatment) motivated her to change. She transformed the academy into more of a club. Then the field trips were no longer seen as exclusionary; rather, the whole endeavor became extracurricular. Suits were not mandatory; instead the students wore blazers on their outings to show solidarity.

This by no means diminished the importance of her honors academy. Her students went on to earn hundreds of thousands of dollars in scholarship money and were among the first in their families to attend and graduate from college. The takeaway is that the mismatch in perspectives—in this case, a biased perception—nearly thwarted her efforts just because she initially imposed her own belief system on her students.

DETERMINE IF YOU BRING A BIAS INTO THE INTERACTION

When interacting with students, think of their individual perspectives and how they compare with your own. For example, let's say one of your students is chronically late for school. You may have many different feelings and reactions, depending on your perspective. You may feel like the student isn't taking attendance seriously or is being disrespectful. That is an unintentional bias. You are drawing certain assumptions based on the student's actions that are being fueled by your beliefs and attitudes about what it takes to be a good student. Now consider this counternarrative: There may be circumstances that cause the student to be late every day. For many urban students who reside in low-income families and have no choice but to work to help provide for their family, just the act of coming to school is an accomplishment. The self-examination that Freire emphasized begins with working on our own biases to interact with others from a more understanding place.

Your bias, shaped by your own life experiences—experiences that are likely very different from your student's—informed your judgment. Tardiness is often perceived as a lack of commitment, a lack of respect, or disinterest on the part of the student, but what if your student has no choice but to walk miles to school?

The perspective of most educators is that we want the student to embrace the concept that school is a place for learning—a priority. But from the student's perspective, this may not jive with *their* immediate priorities. Those who grow up in circumstances similar to my own experience success in different ways: Simply having enough money to pay all your bills and eat may be the priority and be equated with success.

Well-known psychologist Albert Bandura's social learning theory claims children pay close attention to behaviors around them. According to Bandura, "Most human behavior is learned observationally through modeling from others" (Learningtheories.com 2020). Some of these influences can be quite positive, but others might be damaging. As they are growing, children imitate the behaviors copied from their surroundings.

KIDS BENEFIT FROM OBSERVATIONAL LEARNING

Working, or *hustling*, is what many of your students have seen and modeled. Hustling, or making money by any means, is learned behavior, but you don't have to go to school to learn it. Hustling can take many forms and not all of them are illicit or harmful. Many successful adults attribute their perseverance and work ethic to early experiences that may not have conformed to middle-class values.

A child's notion of success is formed by that child's experiences. For some children, car ownership may be a symbol of success, whether or not the car owner ever finished high school. If we work to broaden a child's exposure to new phenomena, we stand a better chance of broadening the child's perspective. Something as simple as a college visit, a field trip, or exposure to successful mentors who grew up in a similar background provide students with opportunities to observe people who look like them and who are engaged in meaningful work and appealing activities that they never believed would be open to them.

I want to challenge a common stereotype that most children who don't see the value of school are Black or Brown. However, few can deny the history of public schooling in the United States reveals a pattern of inequitable opportunities for students of color. With that said, I can recall one of my white students who did not feel that school was important because her mom, a high school dropout, earned over $1,900 a week as a bartender. Clearly, in this child's experience, one could be successful and live a good life without a high school diploma. Yet by broadening this child's experience through exposure to a variety of alternatives we can potentially open her mind to different perspectives on the value of school.

➡ EXPOSURE INFLUENCES PERSPECTIVE

I grew up in a family of hustlers. My mom and dad both had a gambling addiction. It should come as no surprise that when I went to school, my biggest drive was to acquire wealth. I can remember the biggest arguments between my mom and my sister invariably centered on money. My mom would let my sister know that "you have to get out there and work because nobody is gonna give you anything." The messages we received were limited to the reality that we needed to make money to survive. Just to be clear, my intent is not to fault my parents, much in the way that I discourage educators from blaming parents for *their* children's poor attendance or lack of commitment to school. My parents were just living the way they were raised. And, in all fairness, they weren't kidding: We really *did* need that money to survive.

Again, I want to reinforce that exposure to different experiences and ways of life can open our minds to new possibilities. Once you learn that your students have not been exposed to simple things, such as the mall on the other side of town, or a live theatrical or musical performance, or even an animal other than a dog, cat, or squirrel up close—or seen a person of color wear a suit and tie—then you can begin to plan ways to expose them to more. There is no way we can change our students' adverse childhood experiences (a topic that is covered later in this book), but we can shape who they become by exposing them to a range of novel experiences.

➡️ MENDING A GET-BY MENTALITY

Tap into your students' interests and expose them to new possibilities in life. Once I understood that I had students who loved to write, I took them to poetry slams. Their perspectives changed from merely wanting to "get by" to enhanced motivation and aspirations when they saw that their interests could actually produce a beautiful outcome. One of my students had a passion for growing plants outdoors, so I took that student to an agricultural museum. This exposure sparked a realization that a love of something so simple could actually become a meaningful living. I also saw that once my students understood the potential to transform their passions into ways to not only survive but thrive, they would work like crazy to make that happen. Passion feeds motivation, but we must first provide our students with a glimpse into what is possible.

➡️ SEEING WHAT IS BEHIND THE PACKAGE

As a child, my way of being in the world was the hustle. Nobody in my family had ever finished high school. For many years, my perspective was that school had no connection to my survival. Consequently, my approach to school was to just get by. At home we did not talk about school or homework. But I want to again be clear that this is not meant to be a value judgment toward my family or others who live in poverty. A difference isn't the same as a deficit, and our society provides some children with more opportunities and options than others. My view of success and my teachers' view of success were different. I come from a family of survivors—they were forced to work when they were thirteen and fourteen, and school was not part of our narrative. After all, when you don't have the awareness to see that other possibilities exist and there is no food on the table, how can your perspective shift to one that sees the value of a formal education? Similarly, for educators, understanding the *truth behind the package* is the key to establishing a connection with your students. In other words, don't form your judgments based on what you see on the surface.

How often do we judge people based on what we see on the surface—the "package?" Children, like all human beings, are complex, and what we see on the surface can never fully reflect their lived experiences or their potential. For this reason, educators can't possibly shift their students' perspectives without first peeling away the layers to get to what is really inside that package.

Dos and Don'ts

As we close this chapter, we have learned how one's perspective can be enhanced through experiencing situations through the eyes of the student. The checklist below will be followed by a moment to reflect. Remember to be honest with yourself and use this time to create an action plan to enhance your own perspective.

DO:

- Allow your students to elaborate on what has shaped their perspectives.

- Talk with your students about any implicit biases that could possibly affect their educational experience.

- Plan field trips and visits from professionals to expose students to more perspectives and possibilities.

- Try to dig deep to understand what is behind the package.

- Help shift the "get-by" mentality by exposing your students to new environments, possibilities, and ways of being that connect to their interests and passions.

DON'T:

- Assume you know what is best for your students, especially when your interactions are limited to superficial exchanges.

- Expect your students to know about a world outside their neighborhood.

- Assume your vision of success is the same as your student's.

Chapter Reflection

This chapter has encouraged you to enhance your perspective by seeing the world through your students' eyes and being open to their realities. Use the questions below to detail times when you felt you were able to help enhance your perspective along with your students'.

Think about your students. Have you ever honestly taken the time to visit their neighborhoods or examine any cultural nuances they carry into your classroom?

```
_____
_____
_____
_____
```

Was there ever a time when you needed to peel back the layers of a disengaged student to reveal who that student really was? Do you think exposure to other things, such as field trips, could have helped that student find inspiration?

```
_____
_____
_____
_____
```

How does having an understanding of your own biases influence your teaching style?

```
_____
_____
_____
_____
```

CHAPTER 4

Know Their Strengths

Develop Positive Attitudes and Student Growth

Have you ever been in a situation where you constantly thought about an outcome—*really* thought about it and planned every detail—and to your surprise, it actually turned out the way you planned it? That is the power of manifestation through positive thinking. Rhonda Byrne, author of *The Secret*, wrote in her book that thoughts become things. And this can be true in many instances. We recognize that what we look for is what we tend to see. Instead of looking for an outcome that is negative or that contains some flaw, look for something positive that can be beneficial or add to your perspective. By shifting to search for happiness, you can create it.

Byrne also quoted humorist Prentice Mulford, saying, "A person who sets his or her mind on the dark side of life, who lives over and over the misfortunes and disappointments of the past, prays for similar misfortunes and disappointments in the future. If you will see nothing but ill luck in the future, you are praying for such ill luck and will surely get it." This shows how powerful thoughts can be, and expecting a positive outcome will surely enhance the odds that you will achieve it. (p. 177)

The same goes with our kids. Happiness comes when they realize they are good at something. When educators apply a positive lens and identify their students' strengths, the students will work harder to maximize their own potential. I would go so far as to argue that this is the purpose of a school. In the best of worlds, school helps build on students' strengths to the point where they can become better than they were when they arrived. And, of course, when our students benefit, we (the adults in the room) benefit as well.

You can't make positive choices for the rest of your life without an environment that makes those choices easy, natural, and enjoyable. — **Deepak Chopra**

Deepak Chopra gained international acclaim with his efforts to change the world by educating people that making strides in a positive direction can result from changing one's thinking. That can also take some self-reflection: Are we basing our impressions of a student's present self on past negative interactions? If Rhonda Byrne is correct, using past interactions to determine a student's present or even future will only manifest a negative outcome for the student. The more we tend to expect mediocre outcomes, the more likely we are to get exactly that!

◀▶ OUR THOUGHTS BECOME MANIFEST IN A CHILD

I was once on a high school campus for a speaking engagement. While I was engaged in a casual conversation with the principal and a parent, the principal called out to a student and asked him to step up and to shake his hand. The young man looked like he had been awake for days and carried with him a strong smell of drugs; his eyes were also bloodshot. Despite this student's outward appearance, the principal greeted him warmly, shook his hand, and wished him a great day. The parent standing with us was appalled. "Why did you let him in?" he asked, inferring that permitting "that type" of child to come into the school was an abomination. I will never forget that principal's response: "I'm just glad he's here, he could be on the streets." In that moment, I got it. That principal got it. What a clear example of maximizing the positive rather than the more predictable response of spinning into negativity!

Later, the principal explained to me that this student had had an egregious number of absences that school year alone, had a record longer than his arm, and was known for breaking into houses. Showing up in school kept him off the streets and out of trouble.

Try to imagine the life that kid must have had. Many cannot, and many place false expectations on students without giving them the benefit of the doubt. Most students are unfortunately guilty until proven innocent in our school system, and that sets them up for failure. When we learn to view our students through a positive lens, when we identify and articulate the good in that student, we can help the student envision new possibilities and even a whole new life. When the student who smelled like drugs entered the school and was greeted with positive energy rather than accusations and stereotypes, he was able to have a safe and productive day. I later learned that this student graduated high school and now enjoys a stable and meaningful career. I can't say it often enough—perspective matters! Although the student appeared to be destined for failure, the principal was able to see something positive. Maybe the student came to school three times that week whereas he had only attended once the previous week: That's a win. Or maybe he didn't get a write-up that week but in previous weeks he had: That's another win!

Let's stop labeling such students "at risk." Think of it this way: In the absence of the right supports, any of us could be at risk for negative outcomes. To me, that's akin to a self-fulfilling prophecy, one that could influence your teaching style in a manner that doesn't hold your students to a higher standard and instead condemns them to an uncertain future. Rather than dwelling on past experiences, change your lens to one that is focused on the future.

THE PYGMALION EFFECT

In 1968 psychologist and theorist Robert Rosenthal conducted a landmark experiment to see whether student achievement could be impacted by the expectations of their teachers. He speculated that if students were nurtured and told they were smart, they would perform better in school. The experiment showed that teacher expectations worked as a self-fulfilling prophecy. The teachers' expectations altered the way the children were treated, and this affected their abilities. In an article for *Simply Psychology*, Derek Schaedig (2020) summed this up:

> Rosenthal and Jacobsen gave elementary school children an IQ test and then informed their teachers which children were going to be average and which children were going to be "Bloomers", the twenty percent of students who showed "unusual potential for intellectual growth."
>
> They found that the teachers did not expect too much from the average children and gave all the attention to the Bloomers. The teachers created a nicer environment for the Bloomers, they gave them more time and attention, they called on them for answers more often

and they gave them more detailed feedback when they got something wrong.

However, unknown to the teachers, these students were selected randomly and may or may not have fulfilled that criteria. After eight months, they came back and retested the children's intelligence.

Unintentionally, working from a predetermined set of "rules" or assumptions, these teachers devoted more attention and care to students who were portrayed as "above average," and they did so in a markedly different manner from how they treated their "average" or "below average" students. These teachers developed a bias founded on little knowledge of these children other than mere hearsay. And, with that, the students who were treated as "smart" performed better. In the words of teaching expert Jon Saphier (2017), these teachers appeared to have limited awareness that "smart is something you can get."

⏩ PREDETERMINING A STUDENT'S OUTCOME

I've researched many writers and theorists who study student growth and potential. I have been stunned by the amount of literature that attempts to predict which students will and will not be successful. In a 1992 article about the characteristics of at-risk students published by the National Center for Education Statistics, authors Kaufman and Owings summarized how we can place our students at a predetermined disadvantage. They stated that

> an "at-risk" student is generally defined as a student who is likely to fail at school. In this context, school failure is typically seen as dropping out of school before high school graduation. As a result, the characteristics of at-risk students have traditionally been identified through retrospective examinations of high school dropouts' family and school histories. Those characteristics associated with dropping out of school then become the defining characteristics of at-risk students...students are considered at risk of school failure if, in the eighth grade, they had failed to achieve basic proficiency in mathematics or reading, or had dropped out of school altogether. While some proportion of these students may eventually graduate high school with adequate literary and numeracy skills, their academic performance in the eighth grade has put them at risk of school failure. (p. 2)

These findings (and the assumptions upon which they are based) are heartbreaking. They presume that once a child has failed multiple assessments, the inevitable outcome is that child giving up and dropping out. How unfair is that?

Not only are such diminished expectations unjust but they also fail to take into account the complex factors and events that influence our children's lives. What if a kid failed a test because he was having a bad day? (How many of us can honestly state that we don't have bad days?) What if a child is consumed by fears of looming eviction notices and stays focused on hustling to make next month's rent? Think about how hungry he might be because he didn't make it to school in time for breakfast? This is real life for many of our kids, and predicting their futures based on test results does not do them justice. Let's be honest, can a standardized assessment truly measure a child's tenacity or ingenuity for survival in the face of so many adverse circumstances?

THE TROUBLE WITH STANDARDIZED TESTS

Many standardized tests that are used in urban and marginalized populations are developed by people who have no knowledge of the dynamic of this population. The tacit assumption is that all students share the same middle-class values, aspirations, and life experiences. To offer an extreme example, test questions about how many crepe myrtle trees were planted in the nation's capital do not resonate with children who are more concerned about ducking at the sounds of shots as they walk home from school. Moreover, a number of educational researchers have cited evidence that most high-stakes tests are culturally biased, which can set a child up for failure. Authors Shane Safir and Jamila Dugan categorize norm-referenced standardized tests as a form of "satellite data"—data that "hover far above our classrooms and tell a very incomplete story about our students" (p. 56). In their words,

> While satellite data can illuminate trends and point our attention toward underserved groups of students, they have a few fatal flaws...perhaps most problematically, satellite data serve to reinforce implicit biases and deficit thinking about African American, Latinx, and Indigenous students, students with diverse abilities, and other historically marginalized learners. They project a single story about "under-performance" rather than illuminating the complexity of learning and the tremendous

assets that every child brings. By attempting to distill the kaleidoscopic process of learning into a metric and promoting a narrow discourse of achievement, satellite data contribute to a long, racist history of insinuating that students of color have lower intellectual capacity rather than differential access to opportunity. (p. 56)

To put it more succinctly, standardized tests are no indication of a student's capacity to navigate an increasingly complex world. Rather than falling prey to the Pygmalion effect, perhaps you should ask yourself, what exactly are we measuring and why is it relevant to our students' lives?

➡️ RATHER THAN OBSESS OVER TEST SCORES, LOOK FOR POSITIVE STUDENT GROWTH

In the face of an ever-changing world, why would we continue to rely on a fixed-in-time measure that is questionable to begin with? How might this put our most marginalized students at a severe disadvantage by not allowing them to apply their critical-thinking skills to a situation that is more relevant to their own life experiences? A far more useful indicator of progress (as well as our effectiveness as educators) is measuring growth over time. The Texas Education Agency (2016) highlights the importance of student growth by stating that

> student growth measures how much a student progresses academically during his or her time with a particular teacher. It takes into consideration a student's entering skill level when measuring how much the student grew over time, and, as opposed to measuring student proficiency on an assessment, student growth isn't concerned with whether or not a student passes a particular test or reaches a predetermined and uniform benchmark. It considers equally students who enter behind grade level, on grade level, and beyond grade level, tailoring growth expectations to each student's context.

Texas is not alone in prioritizing student growth over a single data point—the results of a standardized test. Think about how a growth model not only better positions students for success but also reinforces teachers' positive perspectives on the potential and capabilities of their students, given the right supports.

Dos and Don'ts

We as educators are frequently challenged to rely on our inherent creativity. We create differentiated lesson plans that meet a variety of learning needs, and we continually refine our practice in response to what we observe and learn when we truly tune into our students. In the spirit of creativity, imagine yourself in a situation that is foreign to you and think about how you'd want to be treated. For example, if you are afraid of heights, think of how well you'd perform on a high wire above a crowd. How might those around you offer reassurance, comfort, and support? Puts things into perspective a little more, doesn't it?

DO:

- Begin each day with a new and positive perspective on all of your students.

- Find at least one positive aspect about a student who challenges you the most and focus on that positive aspect; remind the student of how much you value that aspect of the student's being.

- Focus on the good in your students and celebrate little wins, such as showing up for class on time.

- Focus on student growth and cultural responsiveness in your assessments and take your students' individual life experiences into account when you evaluate their outcomes.

DON'T:

- Assume your students are destined for failure based on their past test results.

- Make surface-level judgments about your students or assume that you can readily identify their needs. Think beyond the package.

- Place so much focus on grades and assessments. They are not an accurate indicator of a child's potential or ingenuity.

- Set your students up for failure by ignoring the good in them.

Chapter Reflection

This chapter was written to help us broaden our perspective by looking closely at a student's lived experiences and using that as a lynchpin to accentuate their positive attributes. When you reflect in the spaces below, be honest with yourself so you can be better for your students.

Think about your students. Describe a time when you used a state-mandated exam to scare a student into doing work. Was that fair to the student? What might have been a different course of action?

```
_____

_____

_____

_____
```

Was there ever a time when you could have found something positive in a student but neglected to recognize or acknowledge that attribute? What is something you wish you could have said to that student?

```
_____

_____

_____

_____
```

With the knowledge you have now, how will you design and utilize assessments for your students in the future?

```
_____

_____

_____

_____
```

CHAPTER 5

Put Yourself in Their Shoes

Understand and Respond to Their Whys

Pencil
I woke myself up
Because we ain't got an alarm clock
Dug in the dirty clothes basket,
Cause ain't nobody washed my uniform
Brushed my hair and teeth in the dark,
Cause the lights ain't on
Even got my baby sister ready,
Cause my mama wasn't home.
Got us both to school on time,
To eat us a good breakfast.
Then when I got to class the teacher fussed
Cause I ain't got no pencil

— *Joshua Dickerson*

This poem went viral when it was tweeted by many people with varying opinions on what is really important in schools and for our kids. Empathy is a great tool for approaching situations from a new angle. We often forget that our own frame of reference, one that is informed by our particular life experiences, is just one among many. By putting yourself in the students' shoes, you're not only broadening your perspective but you're also increasing your ability to connect with your students in an authentic way. In this chapter we will call upon teachers to try on their students' glasses in order to better understand the perspectives of the students and how those perspectives inform their decisions and actions.

➡ MEETING STUDENTS WHERE THEY ARE

I'm reminded of an incident I encountered prior to a speaking engagement at a high school. That morning I stood with the principal at the front door as the students entered the building. Like many modern urban schools, this school made it mandatory for students to walk through metal detectors and also subjected them to mandatory bag searches for possible contraband. A student was accosted as he walked through the metal detector when the security officers found he had a backpack full of candy. When that candy was taken from him, he became frantic, saying how much he needed it.

Despite the presence of security and many bystanders, the young man would not calm down. Once his bag of candy was taken away from him, he became irate to the point that he broke the metal detectors. As he was being escorted out of the school, I approached him, and, after some coaxing, the officers allowed me to talk to him. He explained to me how much he needed that candy because his mom was the so-called Candy Lady. She used what she could of her food stamps to buy candy to sell to the children in his neighborhood. She needed that money to pay her rent. He further explained that he needed the candy because he sold his portion at school so he could make his share of the rent and have a place to live. To him, that candy was not contraband, it was a means of basic survival.

At that point I could empathize with the young man. As I was raised in a household where I was taught that survival and making money were more important than school or anything else, I could relate to his urgency to hold on to his only source of income and his need to have a place to lay his head at night and a roof to cover it. Much like me at his age, schooling and formal education held little value for him. Rather, school was a venue for selling candy and enabling him to help pay bills and live.

➡ MASLOW'S HIERARCHY OF NEEDS

Sometimes it's too easy to overlook the fact that many of our students do not have the means to support some of life's basic needs. I assume that many of my readers are familiar with Maslow's hierarchy of needs from your pre-service course work. In the midst of the COVID-19 pandemic, many educators heard the expression "Maslow over Bloom," a reminder that, under dire circumstances, basic survival needs must take priority over such luxuries as self-actualization. A quick refresher on Maslow: Psychologist and human motivation expert Abraham Maslow, in his landmark 1943 paper "A Theory of Human Motivation," detailed what all people must have in order to fully self-actualize and live to their fullest potential. Maslow elaborated on how if very basic needs such as shelter, food, and safety are not met, people will not have the motivation to do anything other than merely survive. In order to better understand what motivates us, Maslow determined that human needs can be organized into a hierarchy—an order of importance—in which the very basic needs must be met in order for the final step of self-actualization to be reached. According to Maslow, when a lower need is met, we can progress to meeting the next need in the hierarchy.

So, what if basic needs such as food, shelter, and safety are *not* met? As adults, we find it difficult to function without our cell phones, let alone food. And, in the southern United States, where I live, the water pipes burst when the temperature dips below 30°F. In the few days it takes for people to get back their running water, we often experience something akin to anarchy in the streets. This may seem extreme, but the poverty statistics don't lie: This is daily life for a number of our marginalized students. According to a report issued by the Children's Defense Fund in 2020:

- More than 1 in 6 children under six are poor and almost half of them live in extreme poverty.
- Nearly 1 in 3 Black (30.1 percent) and American Indian/ Alaska Native children (29.1 percent) and nearly 1 in 4 Hispanic children (23.7 percent) are poor compared with 1 in 11 white children (8.9 percent).

Much like the poem at the beginning of this chapter, it's quite hard to find relevance in formal schooling when you are reprimanded for not having a pencil, especially when your primary focus is just making it to see another day.

← PUTTING YOURSELF IN THEIR SHOES

You just need to put yourself in someone else's shoes and then see how they feel and then you will understand why they are reacting or why they are behaving the way that they are behaving. We need to be fair. — **Navid Negahban**

As a teacher I once encountered an unusual situation: One of our students showed up late every morning but also left late in the evening. My coworkers and I used to beg him to leave school in the afternoon; part of our job was to clear the school grounds quickly to prevent students from fighting, and this also enabled us to go home at a reasonable hour. I was assigned to monitor the grounds of the school at the end of the day, and I couldn't go home until every student was either picked up or on the school bus. For weeks I pleaded with this student. One night, I jokingly said to him, "Man why do we go through this every day? *Begging* to make you leave?" (I was careful not to show anger and smiled the whole time.) He just laughed, we talked a bit, and he eventually went on his way.

One afternoon I was late leaving school and I rode past the bus stop for the city transportation. I spotted this same student waiting for the bus and pulled over to speak to him. I then noticed he was sitting with a girl who I later learned was his younger sister from the elementary school. So much was going through my head; I felt frustrated but mostly just wanted to know, *why were they here*, just sitting and waiting? The story he told broke me down. He said to me,

> Me and my family stay in a hotel across town. My mother don't have a car to get us to school so we meet her every afternoon at a certain bus stop where she gets on the bus after work. I usually hang out at the school for a while longer because my sister don't get out of her after-school program until like 4:00, and plus I be trying to wait until all the students leave so they wouldn't laugh at me getting on the city bus.

It is important to understand that in our small city, public transportation is typically used by those without cars, those who are homeless. or those who are simply out of luck. In other words, the connotations associated with riding the bus are invariably negative.

I immediately broke down from the realization that my perspective on this young man was negatively biased. Sadly, I had never thought to discover his *why*. Now that I was able to step into his shoes for a few minutes and enhance my perspective, I was able to imagine myself in his situation, trying to keep a low profile at the bus stop out of fear of being judged by his peers. What was more surprising about this story is that he was an honor student who never got in trouble; his only misstep was being tardy. I can only imagine how my misreading of his motivation—a kid who just wanted to hang around after school to cause trouble—impacted his self-esteem. That chance encounter at the bus stop made me aware of his kindness and protectiveness toward his sister as well as the respect he gave his mom. This was a good kid; he could've easily used his situation as an excuse, but he didn't.

If you find it difficult to put yourself in the shoes of a child who is living in radically different circumstances than your own, try the following exercise. Think of a time in your life when *you* had to transition to survival mode. This could range from confronting serious illness, to your memories of having been bullied as a child, to having endured a natural disaster. In the midst of such challenging moments, what ran through your mind? What were your priorities? What was the impact of such hardships on your perspective?

➦ HELPING STUDENTS FIND THEIR MOTIVATION

Motivation is one of the most complex aspects of human experience. I was reminded of this when a friend who taught in an inner-city high school recounted the following story:

> So there was a time when I was working at the high school when I would hold after-school clubs in the library; this year I held the journalism club. The library was the best place for the few of us to have some time to talk about writing and what stories to publish in the school paper. Well, I noticed one of my students, not somebody who participated in the journalism club, would be there in the library on the computer every day. He always sat at the last computer in the row—out of the way—and with his headphones on just worked. I didn't think much of it, but I noticed every time I was in the library, he was too. When I would stop by to chat after school with my friend who was the librarian at the time, he'd be there. Now, for the sake of this story, let's call this kid Marcus. Marcus was amazing in class—sweet, did his work—but he was even more amazing on the football field. Now, this high school had by no means a Heisman-winning team, but the points the school did score were scored by Marcus, so he was a really stellar player. Well, one day, after seeing this student in the library for weeks, I stopped by to speak with my friend the librarian. We chatted quite a while and realized it had gotten quite late. We gathered our things and headed to the door, and as my friend turned off the lights, she turned to Marcus and said, "Remember to keep the light off so no one will bother

you. See you tomorrow." Marcus pulled his headphones down and said sweetly, "Yes ma'am." Of course I was intrigued and asked my friend why Marcus was in the library every day. Well, my friend divulged to me that Marcus was one of eight children and he lived with all seven of his siblings (his mother was incarcerated), his aunt, and three or four other cousins in a two-bedroom, one-bathroom apartment over an old mill that had no running water. Hearing this stunned me! The librarian then went on to tell me that Marcus worked on the computer to apply to colleges and write to football scouts. I thought that was amazing but did not know why that would take him late into the evening, so I asked if he stayed that late every day. My friend then told me that Marcus stayed past 5:00 p.m. every day because that was the time one of the businesses downtown near his apartment closed, at which time Marcus and his brothers would fill buckets and bottles of water using the business's outside hose. I was literally amazed at how this kid, an eleventh grader, still came to school, still applied to colleges, still worked in class, but did not even have running water at home. He needed the buckets to flush the toilet, which they only flushed once a day. He needed the water to fill the sink for all twelve or thirteen of his family members to wash up for the next day. He needed the water to drink and to cook and to make formula for his baby cousin. I was even more struck when my friend said, as we both got into our nice cars, "He's dealing with more than I could imagine, the least I can do is let him stay in a safe place until after 5:00 p.m. I had to put myself in his shoes—I had to think what would I resort to if I were in his situation and felt my back was against the wall."

Many of us find such a life experience unthinkable. Living without basic needs and still having the fortitude to try to better your situation is a big deal. I am happy to say that Marcus was recruited by several top colleges and earned a full scholarship. He is working and thriving and also taking good care of his siblings. But what if he had been discouraged by that librarian? What if he had not had the opportunity to provide clean water to his family? These *what ifs* are what keep me and many others awake at night. These are the real-life scenarios that confront all too many of our students every day. Yet educators have the power to help shape positive outcomes for students, even those who are faced with dire circumstances. But first we must take the time and effort to understand our students' lived experiences and get in touch with their *whys*.

GIVE KIDS MORE OPTIONS

There are many people who work hard to help our students thrive even when the cards seem to be stacked against them. A principal at the lowest-ranked high school in my state started a night school for overaged and undercredited students. He recognized the need because he understood that these students either worked during the day or had to take care of their families. Night school was just a better option for them. Instead of foregoing their education altogether in order to fulfill their basic needs, they were able to work at their own pace in the evening and still take care of all their business during the day. This is the type of creative and out-of-the-box thinking that enables our kids who have been labeled "at risk" to thrive.

Dos and Don'ts

We can enhance our perspectives by putting ourselves in a student's shoes. There have surely been times where you have needed someone to show you some understanding. That simple act of empathy can go a long way toward uplifting a student. Use these Dos and Don'ts to replace your current thinking.

DO:

- Look at the multiple creative ways you can handle challenging situations with your students before writing them off as "at risk."

- Get in touch with your students' lived experiences, not by being nosy, but by observing and asking the right questions or simply letting them vent to you.

- Give students more options to access their education.

DON'T:

- Chastise a student over simple things, such as not having supplies, when you do not know what is going on at that student's home.

- Force students to forgo their innate urge to fulfill basic needs by insisting that they prioritize their lessons over their survival and that of their family.

Chapter Reflection

This chapter has allowed us to think more deeply about what is going on in our students' lives by allowing ourselves to refocus and broaden our perspectives and step into the students' shoes. To one person, a child may seem aloof, when in actuality, that child may be thinking about how they are going to get home or how they are going to provide water to their siblings. Use the reflection area to dig deeper into how you can help build a student toward self-actualization.

When you think about your students, think of one who you know is struggling with basic needs. How can you help that student?

_____

_____

_____

_____

What additional options can you give your students to help increase their motivation?

_____

_____

_____

_____

With the knowledge you have now, how will you look at your students when they are late or do not compete an assignment? How can you refocus those students to rise above their personal situations and thrive?

_____

_____

_____

_____

CHAPTER 6

Show Them You Care

Create Safe Spaces and Build Trust

Marcus Garvey was born in Jamaica and immigrated to the United States early in his life. Garvey took on the mission of educating marginalized populations of color (then and now among our nation's most vulnerable populations) and striving for equity. As an activist in the early 1900s, he was acutely aware of the inequities that had plagued these communities for generations. As most seasoned educators have learned, in order to build up a child's capacity to learn, we must first give that child the confidence to know that they *can* learn. Why? Because when a child has been relegated to living in the margins and has often been failed by the education system, that child will develop a sense of distrust. And, as we learned in the first half of this book, most children who have only experienced life in the margins simply can't envision other options. In many of his lectures, Garvey summarized his views on the rights of African Americans by noting, "The first dying that is to be done by the Black man in the future will be done to make himself free" (Van Leeuwen 2000). Some might find Garvey's beliefs extreme, but his essential message is about supporting and uplifting marginalized people of color by opening their eyes to the possibility of a life worth living and a world in which they can thrive. Creating opportunities for such exposure will help to form and shape students' perspectives.

LIVED EXPERIENCES

Students' perspectives are formed throughout their lives based on factors such as family, community, peers, culture, education, and other life experiences. Take a moment to consider the influences on your students' perspectives apart from school. Even students growing up in the most challenging of circumstances can have very positive role models, such as community and religious leaders and strong parental figures who model positive work ethics. They may experience an array of rich cultural traditions that will serve them well across their life spans. The key is not to pass judgment on or attempt to erase these influences but rather to reinforce the importance of exposing our students to a myriad of experiences and opportunities in life, many of which can only be attained through a formal education. We can affirm our students' identities while at the same time broadening their perspectives. Throughout this chapter we will discuss ways to build students' trust as a prerequisite to broadening their perspectives.

SOCIAL COGNITIVE THEORY

Albert Bandura, the esteemed social psychologist who was introduced in Chapter 3, is well-known for a theory that details how youth obtain knowledge through their interactions with others. Social cognitive theory, which is used in psychology, education, and communication, holds that portions of an individual's knowledge acquisition can be directly related to observing others within the context of social interactions, experiences, and outside media influences. This includes teachers. Teachers spend a good deal of time with their students, so never think that you, as an educator, do not have the ability to shape and ultimately change lives. But you have to break down a few proverbial walls first to build that trust up within the student population you serve. Building a foundation of trust will come only after a child feels safe enough to connect with you.

WHEN YOU REMODEL A HOUSE, YOU MUST KNOCK DOWN SOME WALLS FIRST

If you have ever made updates to your home or seen design shows on TV, you understand that you must first tear down old walls and floors to get that new, desired outcome. The same applies to your students. These metaphorical walls are those they have constructed to prevent others from getting close to them. Think of the floors as the weakened foundation—the deficit narratives that have led them to think that they will never succeed in school or that school is of no value to people like them. The trick is to build them up with encouragement that is not forced but is genuine and full of grace.

What the eyes see, and the ears hear, the mind believes. — **Harry Houdini**

Harry Houdini was best known for his magic and sleight of hand moves that shocked audiences in the early 1900s. He was also extremely popular for his escape acts. He could convince the audience into believing that they were seeing the unbelievable. He seemingly escaped death doing some of the most crazy things—so much so that some people thought he had sold his soul just to captivate an audience. In actuality, he allowed his audience to believe the story he created. We may not be magicians, but as educators we can do the same: captivate our students so much so that they begin to believe a new narrative, one that is uplifting. One that says they can achieve anything in spite of very real obstacles and structural inequities—even things that may seem impossible. It all starts with getting your students' minds to wrap around the idea that you actually care and can actually help them transcend their difficult life circumstances.

Start by getting in touch with your students' interests. These can vary widely and may include books, music, athletic pursuits, gaming, or science, all of which can influence their emergent perspectives. Other influences might be coming from television, social media, and radio. And, of course, family members and peers have influence. I've already disclosed my own life experience in which my parents valued earning money above all else—something that seemed incompatible with doubling down on my formal education. But consider the source of such values and belief systems. People who have been historically marginalized and denied access to a quality education may have good reason to distrust or lose faith in our educational institutions. And this lack of trust can endure across generations.

As a child I was taught to be a fighter and not let someone "punk" me. This stance was a mode of survival in my neighborhood. If you displayed any sign of weakness or fear, you were labeled as "lame" and kids would bully you. I learned to be aggressive, even if that was against my nature. Unfortunately, this dynamic hasn't changed a great deal since my childhood. I've observed too many kids from backgrounds like mine who feel the only way to solve a problem is through aggression. Such aggression can be triggered by even the slightest provocation, and some children simply can't control their impulse to fight. Chances are you've encountered children like me over the course of your teaching career. How much influence did you feel you had on them, and what did you do to earn their trust?

If a person has your ear, they have your influence — **Bishop T. D. Jakes**

Have you ever felt as if you had no influence over your students? Let's think about how this puts you, the educator, at a disadvantage. When the going gets tough, our tendency is to fall back on the rules we've devised. For example, *if someone hits you, walk away from the fight or go tell an adult.* Thinking back to my own childhood, such a rule would have seemed absurd when my very survival depended upon fighting back. Let's be real! Even adults may have difficulty walking away from conflict. Think about the people you work with: How often have you encountered a colleague who simply couldn't let you just walk away if he felt like you wronged him in any way? Now think about your own childhood: When somebody hit you, did *you* walk away? I'm sure I wasn't the only child whose parents told me that the appropriate response was to fight back. And such messages aren't limited to those living in low-income households. How many affluent parents spend a fortune on martial arts classes for their children for this very reason?

SO THIS GOES TO SHOW US THAT MERELY TEACHING RULES IS INEFFECTIVE; RATHER, WE MUST TEACH PRINCIPLES

For many of our students, showing signs of weakness or vulnerability goes against everything they've learned to survive. They live in fear of the consequences of exposing any weakness. Such consequences include bullying, shaming, and physical harm in schools and in neighborhoods. I recently watched a YouTube video of a kid that followed the rule: He walked away from a fight to inform an adult, and other kids hit him all the way down the hall as he cried. The video went viral, and the kid later committed suicide. From this you can understand why, in a world in which humiliation can spread virally over social media, our kids might be resistant to becoming the model students that we would like them to be. Mind you, I fully understand why rules are put in place. My purpose is only to sensitize educators to the very real barriers that keep some of our students from adhering to those rules. We teach students from 8:00 a.m. to 3:00 p.m., but they will always have to return to their neighborhoods by themselves. When children live in fear for their own physical safety, whose rules are they going to follow, yours or the street's?

I remember one day on my morning duty post in front of the school, I watched a kid get out of a car looking very neat, with his shirt tucked in nicely. He kissed his mother on the cheek and told her he loved her. When she said, "Have a great day," he replied, "Yes, ma'am."As soon as she pulled off and he made it to me at the front door, he pulled his pants down and untucked his shirt. I told him, "No, sir," and instructed him to pull his pants back up. I went on to tell him, "I saw what you just did." Although I admonished him I also understood that he was getting ready to walk into an environment in which feeling safe depended upon his ability to fit in with the others.

SO HOW DO WE BREAK THIS BARRIER?

I wish I could provide you with a silver bullet response, but the sources of such barriers, including poverty and adverse childhood experiences, are too big for educators alone to address. But what we *can* do is provide a space in the school where kids don't feel they have to be tough or, for our male students, succumb to toxic masculinity just to fit in. Part of building trust is providing children with a safe and supportive environment in which they needn't fear having their cell phone (or candy for the rent money) confiscated (Hammond 2015). When a child reverts to fight or flight mode—or what author Zaretta Hammond (2015) calls an "amygdala highjack"—your math lesson, no matter how well designed, will have little resonance.

HOW DO WE BUILD TRUST?

Building trust means you allow the students to know that you support them, even in small ways. Ways to accomplish this include tuning into their interests; going to games to show support; asking the right questions; showing concerns about their lives in and out of school; being a father figure, mother figure, or mentor to them; or providing emotional support. The most important thing is *staying consistent*. You can't build trust if you only do these things for a few months and stop. If you begin to earn their trust but then change course, your kids will feel betrayed and it will be even harder to regain that trust.

IN ORDER TO LEAD THEM OUT, YOU MUST ENTER THEIR WORLDS

I love the movie *Lean on Me*. Admittedly, Principal Joe Clark doesn't always do things the right way, but you can't say his heart isn't with those kids. He chains the doors to keep drug dealers out, he fights for his students, and he makes sure everyone is safe in his school. What I love the most, however, is the relationship he has with a young girl named Kaneesha. If you haven't already seen this movie, I urge you to check it out!

One day, as Mr. Clark passes her in the hallway, he notices that Kaneesha is crying. He asks her what is wrong, and her response always cuts right through me: "My mother don't want me anymore." We can't expect our children to enter our classrooms every day completely unburdened, and some students bear extremely heavy loads that some of us can't even imagine. But, as you experience the sadness of the moment, don't miss this important point: Kaneesha isn't alone; she knows that Mr. Clark will be that shoulder she can cry on, because to her, he is the only father figure she has.

RELATIONSHIP BUILDING

Building relationships based on trust is the key to being an influencer. Do you have a relationship with your students like the one Mr. Clark has with Kaneesha? If not, you will encounter difficulty breaking down the barriers that are holding your students back. Watch what happens next in the film. Joe Clark doesn't say, "Let me go find you some help," or throw the problem on someone else. Instead, he enlists his trusted assistant principal, someone who makes decisions with him, and the two of them go to Kaneesha's house to have a talk with her family. They show no hesitation venturing into Kaneesha's low-income neighborhood, which some people call "The Hood." They go directly to the girl's building and tell her mother how important her role is in her daughter's success. In the course of the conversation, the mom reveals that she gave birth to Kaneesha at a young age and subsequently developed a drug habit. Now in recovery, she no longer likes herself and doesn't want Kaneesha to see her in the state she's in. Clark and his AP ask her if they can help her find a job and get her some assistance. This simple interaction helps repair the relationship between mother and daughter, and Kaneesha is invited to move back in.

HARSH TRUTHS AND BRIGHT FUTURES

As an educator, you are responsible for your students' welfare. In truth, not every influencer in a child's life is positive. Some who have watched *Lean on Me* call Principal Clark's management style tyrannical. However, the school he took over was plagued by violence, drug dealing, and gang activity—powerful negative influencers. If we allow these things to go on around us and we don't speak up, we are just as complicit in condemning a child to a bleak future.

Our students can tell the difference between a bystander who simply shows up and collects a paycheck and an actualizer who, like Houdini, can convince us to believe in a new narrative. Try to imagine if students felt like their biggest supporters in the world were their teachers. What if students couldn't wait to come to your class? What if students couldn't wait to jump into your lessons? Just imagine how this would be. How might this change their negative perspectives on school? I have met many amazing teachers who, like magicians, have convinced their students to believe in a brighter future. The great thing about perspective is that, with the right influencers, it is highly malleable.

Circle back to Abraham Maslow's hierarchy of needs. I remember watching an episode of the *Ellen DeGeneres Show* that featured a highly effective principal from New Jersey. This principal knew exactly what Maslow was talking about with regard to providing for basic needs before one could build trust with a student. Jongsma (2018) wrote in his article that the principal, Akbar Cook, had been offered $50,000 by Cheerios in part because he had added washers and driers to his Newark school's campus for student use. In his first year, officials informed him that many students were absent because they didn't have clean clothes to wear and were subsequently bullied for it. In his appearance on the show he emphasized how happy he was to lead his school in providing such a service: "I'm so happy to lead kids that look like me, that sound like me... We are really laying the foundation for what a community school looks like."

Principals like this warm my heart. They get it. They get how hard it is for a child who comes to school with dirty clothes or who can't make the money for rent. Having this capacity for empathy and compassion builds a safe space for kids to thrive and to ultimately trust you.

Dos and Don'ts

This chapter has allowed us to see the importance of being able to build trust between you and your students. This is a huge concept and a goal that is not always easily accomplished, especially with children who have been raised to be survivors. Follow the Dos and Don'ts then reflect on some of your own practices.

DO:

- Create a safe place at school where kids can show up as their full selves and do not have to be anyone else.

- Make principles be the driving force when communicating with students.

- Allow yourself to go outside of your own comfort zone. Make a home visit if you see fit; this will help you connect with your students.

- Start off small with trust and try things such as supporting your students' sporting activities.

DON'T:

- Pass off students who you find challenging to someone else.

- Write off a child's actions as being negative or willful when those actions can be a point of survival.

- Make your school a place where students are afraid to open up to you.

Chapter Reflection

This chapter has allowed us to think about how being an educator can be difficult but also provides a chance for us to make good connections. Building that trust within your students can allow them to thrive and provide a safe space for them to learn in a healthy environment. Use the following to reflect on some practices that you have used or can use to connect and build trust.

When it comes to your educational practices, are you a practitioner of peace? Are you able to help your students break down barriers? How?

_____

_____

_____

_____

In what ways do you support your students outside of the classroom? In what ways can you do more?

With the knowledge you have now, how will you approach students from different backgrounds in order to help them fit in? How will you provide a safe space for them to thrive?

CHAPTER 7

Get Them Moving

Engage Them With Kinesthetic and Collaborative Learning

We expect kids to learn the way we teach when we should teach the way they learn. — ***Anonymous***

If you have ever been to Canada, you may have noticed that large numbers of Canadians appear to be quite physically fit. Obesity seems to be far less prevalent than in the United States, and, even in inclement weather, you may catch of sight of runners and cyclists burning their calories on city streets. Canada's free and universal healthcare is clearly a factor, but a lesser-known fact is that kinesiology is one of the popular majors offered at most Canadian universities. Kinesiology is the scientific study of human or nonhuman body movement. It has a useful purpose. We study kinesiology to improve performance by learning how to analyze the movements of the human body and discover their underlying principles. The study of kinesiology is an essential part of the educational experience of students of physical education, dance, acting, sport, and physical medicine (Neumann 2016).

Canadians who are well versed in kinesiology have a deep understanding of the ways in which movement helps them to learn better. For some American educators who have been brought up in a culture that traditionally values students seated in orderly rows, passively absorbing knowledge, the idea that movement can actually help many students learn may cause cognitive dissonance. But before dismissing it, try to keep an open mind to the science of kinesthetic learning.

KINESTHETIC LEARNING

When teaching, it is important to understand the most effective ways your students learn to retain information and to recognize they have deep knowledge of concepts that they can later transfer to real-life experiences. Undoubtedly, some students are able to learn from what we think of as a traditional approach that includes worksheets, lecture-style lessons, etc. However, as most seasoned educators have learned, far too many cannot. Augmenting your instruction with visual tools such as thinking maps can certainly help improve access to the curriculum for some students. In a similar vein, think of incorporating opportunities for movement into your instruction as a different form of scaffolding.

Macmillian (2018) details the importance of kinesthetic learning by placing it among three core learning styles. The other two are "auditory" and "visual." Think, for instance, of reading instructions or hearing instructions, then performing a proposed task. As opposed to those, kinesthetic learning is concerned with experiences like learning to kick a soccer ball or balancing on a balance beam. We could describe how to perform these activities, but they are typically best learned through activity. As Macmillan formulates it, kinesthetic learners need "a multi-sensory learning environment" and active engagement because movement, trial and error, and other kinds of physical activity help them remember and recall what they know.

While some researchers have recently critiqued the concept of learning styles (May 2018), I can safely state that in my own experience, using kinesthetic learning techniques in education—particularly when teaching underserved youth—significantly increased my students' access to the curriculum. Kinesthetic activities help ingrain learning into long-term memory by turning a lesson into a physical experience. When a child is engaged in a kinesthetic activity, that child is moving and touching and interacting with the lesson. And a great side benefit is that kinesthetic learning activities are usually lots of fun.

MARGINALIZED STUDENTS AND KINESTHETIC LEARNING

I flash back to my time working at a middle school when I taught several students who had a pattern of office referrals and suspensions for exhibiting behavior that my teacher colleagues felt was distracting. When I would talk to these students after they were put out of class, they would lament, "I can't just sit down all day." That got me to thinking: How many students really enjoy sitting all day? For that matter, how many adults like to sit still all day? Not many. Being sedentary for the bulk of the day forced my students to find distractions out of sheer boredom, which then labeled them as a problem.

Researchers agree there are several characteristics that are helpful to look for when identifying a learner who potentially can benefit from kinesthetic learning. These individuals:

- evidence deeper learning when offered the opportunity to learn through hands-on experiences
- become easily bored in a traditional classroom
- learn through movement
- enjoy sports and physical activity
- are active participants rather than passive observers when learning
- enjoy opportunities to go on excursions or be outside the classroom
- like to build things and work with their hands
- love testing things and experimenting and creating
- are restless when they are sedentary
- are natural hand talkers and expressive in general
- love to try new things and rely on what they can experience or perform

I can't tell you how many times I have had conversations with other teachers who have heard their urban and marginalized students express the need to move more in class. Others have told me about students who were motivated to come to school by the promise of gym class or the opportunity to participate on a sports team. Instead of just kicking students out of class when they are moving too much, or doodling on their papers, or getting out of their seats, think about some of the following strategies to keep them engaged through movement.

ENGAGING THROUGH KINESIOLOGY

Earlier in this chapter, we learned that kinesiology is a popular major at many universities in Canada. Similarly, Canadian universities often teach their future educators how to incorporate movement across their curriculum. This type of scaffolding can often change the perspective of your most disengaged students. An article by Child1st Publications (Major 2016) introduced me to a number of useful practices that help these students, some of which are covered in the following section.

GIVE THEM PLENTY OF OUTDOOR TIME

What happens to children when they encounter trees and greenery? When occurs when they go for a brief nature walk, learn lessons outdoors, observe wildlife, or simply relax in front of a nature scene? Such experiences can be exhilarating, fun, and inspirational. For many people they are an essential part of life. We owe children access to nature. In one study of eleven-year-olds living in a British city, researchers monitored how kids spent their time each day after school. Most kids spent less than thirty minutes outside during after-school hours (Cooper et al. 2010).

In another survey of preschools in Ohio, half the children in full-day daycare spent less than twenty-three minutes each day outdoors. One in three kids spent *no* time outdoors (Copeland et al. 2016). We might revise our outlook on where we educate our children once we understand that giving a child the opportunity to learn in nature can be the key to helping change that child's perspective. Exposure to natural settings can even help kids cope with stress. Kids can learn to appreciate nature and be a part of something bigger than their neighborhood.

LET THEM MOVE!

Students may learn more quickly and effectively if you let them stand at their desk, swing their legs, pace the floor—as long as they are not disrupting other students. Nina Fiore (2014) stated that "regular movement has been shown to increase focus and retention in children and adults of all ages. Movement also helps all children regulate (i.e., adjust their energy), and it therefore has been shown to lower rates of behavioral problems such as fighting and bullying."

I once worked with a teacher who had a brilliant idea for her journalism class—she asked her students to interview one other member of the school community every Friday. However, there were qualifiers to being eligible to complete this assignment: Students were required to have attended the journalism class all week (or have an excused absence), and they had to have a clean record (e.g., no behavioral infractions or unexcused absences in their other courses). If they met these criteria, they were free to walk around the building and conduct interviews with teachers, students, custodians, or other support staff. The experiment proved to be a great success, and the journalism teacher's class participation rate shot up. The student reporters spent the beginning part of the following week analyzing their interviews and compiling information on their interviewees. They then presented their reports to the class on the following Wednesday —another opportunity for movement. Thursday was reserved for preparing the next day's interviews. The secret to this teacher's success? She let the students move! Even though they were not sitting at their desks, they were being offered an opportunity for critical thinking, and they began to excel in their other classes just by being present.

BREAK LONG LESSONS INTO SMALLER CHUNKS

The simple act of changing the learning location (have students sit on the rug, learn in stations, go outdoors, or simply change seats) and letting kids experience something new and hands-on is a major principle of kinesthetic learning. As an adult, I find it hard to sit and listen to the same topic for days and days. Anyone who has ever taught a unit on *The Mill on the Floss* can attest that these lessons can lose a student's interest after day three! Break long units up into manageable goals so that once a student has met a certain mark, that student can engage in a project or a mini-presentation. Chunking content and punctuating it with action assignments will help gain and hold a student's attention.

WHEN A FIELD TRIP ISN'T AN OPTION, HAVE STUDENTS IMAGINE THEMSELVES TRAVELING THROUGH A VIRTUAL FIELD TRIP

While it may not actively engage students in movement, a virtual field trip is an amazing way to expose children to places and spaces that they never could have imagined. A virtual field trip is a guided exploration through the World Wide Web that organizes a collection of pre-screened, thematically based web pages into a structured online learning experience. There are tons of free sites online; all that is needed is access to an Internet-enabled computer. And if kids do not have access to a computer or broadband (despite the rise of remote learning due to COVID, the digital divide is still a reality), the teacher can project the images on a screen in class. In either case, teachers can engage students in lively discussions, stimulate their imaginations, and offer them the opportunity to experience the world from their desks.

THEIR ATTENTION FOLLOWS THEIR HANDS

Encourage your students to draw sketches or diagrams of what they are hearing about in a lesson, or, during a math class, teach them to point to each problem they land on. You can also encourage them to use flashcards to practice and reinforce their learning. Not only are you offering options for using their hands to encourage tactile engagement with the content but you are also teaching them to maintain their own space for learning.

SOCIAL LEARNING EXERCISES FOR STUDENTS

Influential psychologist Lev Vygotsky (1978) stressed the importance of social interaction in cognitive development. As might be expected, social interaction also plays an important role in students' outlook on school. Offering the opportunity for such interaction can enhance a child's sense of safety and also help to build long-lasting friendships. A student's positive perspective toward education can broaden due to healthy relationships with peers as well as enhanced opportunities for learning through more hands-on activities. An absence of engagement, compounded with social isolation, reinforces the perception that school is "boring." When we combine opportunities for healthy social interaction with kinesthetic learning, we increase our potential to shift student perspectives all the more. After all, why *shouldn't* school be fun?

A healthy alternative to learning in isolation is participation in a cohort. Having students work in the same team over a period of time (ideally with the participation of families) not only reinforces their pride as a collective (call it *team spirit*) but also helps build trust between team members. All members are accountable for one another, so the kids who form the cohort will be more reluctant to engage in behavior that upsets the flow of the team. This type of learning style gives the students more ownership and teaches them principles; what one does affects the whole because all have a common goal.

I was part of a cohort in my PhD program. Our cohort functioned almost as a family. If one person fell behind, we all fell behind. We frequently collaborated on projects together in hotel rooms, working well into the early mornings until everyone was on the same page. Our shared accountability to one another permitted us to bond in the manner of a family and we ultimately become accountable for our own learning. Our assignments tackled complex issues and came with strict deadlines. However, rather than being constrained within a classroom, we were at liberty to complete these assignments collaboratively, within our own chosen spaces.

The key takeaway from this chapter is get to know your students and offer them a range of learning opportunities including kinesthetic options. Not only will your students learn but you will as well. And it's healthy to remind yourself of why you committed to your chosen field...I suspect that at least one of your reasons was to build and foster positive interactions among your students.

Dos and Don'ts

This chapter has emphasized that children learn in different ways. For some children, incorporating opportunities for movement and healthy peer-to-peer interactions can be a key to broadening their perspectives.

DO:

- Plan to take your classroom to locations outside the school walls.

- Build movement opportunities into your instruction to reach the learners who benefit from a more hands-on experience.

- Create lessons that force kids to explore a world that is outside of their normal perspective.

- Adapt cohort (or team) models to make kids work collaboratively. Remember that collaboration is an essential skill in the twenty-first-century workplace.

DON'T:

- Insinuate students are a problem when they cannot sit still; learning rarely takes place during a CT scan.

- Expect your students to learn in a vacuum. Healthy social interactions can actually enhance learning.

- Consign students to the same place physically all day in the same class.

Chapter Reflection

Being an educator is a position in which one must wear many hats. Being responsible for another person's life and ultimate mental freedom can be stressful at times, but you are here for a reason: The passion you have as an educator will shape and save lives. Reflect on that while thinking of creative strategies you can use in your classes.

When was the last time you planned an activity that required you and your students to move around? How successful was it and what could have made it better?

Have you ever penalized a student for being fidgety or for moving around without permission? How has your perspective about that student changed after reading this chapter?

With the knowledge you now have, how can you introduce a more kinesthetic style into your lessons?

CHAPTER 8

Your Students Will Teach You

Connect With Culturally Responsive Teaching

Culture is central to learning. Scholar and author Geneva Gay (2018), wrote that

> culture is at the heart of all we do in the name of education, whether that is curriculum, instruction, administration, or performance assessment....Culture refers to a dynamic system of social values, cognitive codes, behavioral standards, world views, and beliefs used to give order and meaning to our own lives as well as the lives of others. (p. 8)

Dr. Gay further describes culturally responsive pedagogy as follows:

> Culturally responsive pedagogy validates, facilitates, liberates, and empowers ethnically diverse students by simultaneously cultivating their cultural integrity, individual abilities, and academic success. It is anchored on four foundational pillars of practice—teacher attitudes and expectations, cultural communication in the classroom, culturally diverse content in the curriculum, and culturally congruent instructional strategies. (p. 44)

I would add to Dr. Gay's description that culturally responsive pedagogy plays a role not only in strengthening teaching and learning but also in shaping the perspectives of your students. When you apply innovative, culturally responsive strategies, your students will become more engaged and will begin to understand and appreciate different viewpoints on the value of school.

I can honestly say that growing up I was not exposed to many Black male doctors. I am excited that my daughters now have the opportunity to see dedicated professionals who look like them: Black female doctors, Black female news anchors, and even a Black female vice president. Exposure to successful professionals who look like your students—especially professionals who grew up in similar circumstances—can boost student self-esteem and convince them that achieving similar success is within their reach. Whenever possible, I would urge you to provide your students with such exposure by inviting guest speakers into your classroom, pursuing opportunities for mentorships, or assigning projects that require students to interview these professionals.

I once had a colleague—we'll call her Lisa—who had been a teen mom. She was an excellent student who gave birth to her first baby when she was a junior in high school. Lisa hid her condition for as long as she could. Rumors spread among her classmates and teachers, but she never told anyone about her pregnancy. She worried that people would judge her, and, needless to say, they did. Once the rumors were confirmed, those around her expressed their disappointment in her. How could somebody with so much potential make such a "dumb" decision? Lisa felt ashamed and became withdrawn until one day when she had a life-altering conversation with a teacher. She was approached by her biology teacher, who asked her flat out if she was pregnant. Lisa began to tear up and blurted out, "Yes, it's true."

Thinking that the teacher would judge her, Lisa couldn't even make eye contact and instead stared at her feet. The biology teacher took hold of her, stared into her eyes, and said, "I don't care who thinks what of you. You are always going to be amazing. I also had my first baby when I was very young, so I know what you're going through. And if you ever need a break, come to my class." The biology teacher had a private area behind her classroom where she kept her supplies and biology books. When Lisa felt tired from walking the halls with a pregnant belly, she retreated into that back room, and that is where she developed a fascination for the model skeleton, books, and other items she discovered.

Lisa proved the naysayers wrong. She had her baby, a beautiful little girl, and continued to persevere with her school work. She graduated fourth in her class and earned a full scholarship to college, majoring in—you guessed it—biology! The kind act of a teacher who recognized this young lady's potential and who also had experienced her struggle firsthand sparked a passion inside of Lisa. She is now an extremely successful doctor with hundreds of patients.

Imagine the impact of this experience on a young girl who had been shunned by her peers. Imagine the shock of discovering that a respected elder had at one time been in the exact same predicament. The teacher not only formed a powerful connection with her student but actually changed the course of her life. Such is the power of cultural relevance.

That is the ultimate question for all of us: Do our actions reflect our values? Do our traditions reflect our beliefs? Do our purchases reflect our ethics? After all, what's the point in having values if we don't manifest them in our behavior? — **Colleen Patrick-Goudreau**

Students filter everything through the lens of their personal history and their beliefs, motivations, and personal truths. In this chapter we will discuss strategies that help students broaden their perspective through culturally responsive pedagogy.

When I was pursuing my doctorate, I had a long dialogue about culturally responsive pedagogy with one of my cohort members. She was a young teacher with great energy who, coincidentally, taught at the same school in which I had previously worked. Although we were there at different times, we shared a lot of common stories. Keep in mind, this school had a reputation as a very challenging environment in which to teach. I e-mailed my teacher friend to get her perspective on culturally responsive pedagogy. The remainder of this chapter is devoted to her wise response.

…

I know them culturally—

Understanding the culture and community of students is imperative for success in the classroom. I mean how can you teach them if you can't reach them? My challenge to you as an educator is to become culturally responsive to your students. Learn the foods they eat, the music they listen to and pay attention to the conversations they have. Students are like sponges; they are consuming information every day. It is your job as an educator to be aware and knowledgeable so you can create learning materials and resources that reflect the world as your students see it. Then, and only then, can you challenge them to see the world outside of the one they know.

People would often ask me if I felt "too young" to be in the classroom with middle schoolers—the answer was no. In fact, I felt like being a little closer to them in age allowed me to understand life as they were experiencing it. Even though I'm a millennial, the lifestyle that my Gen-Z students have was incepted during my childhood. So, though I was a decade apart in age, I could still relate.

One of the most important elements of learning is communication. In this case, we're discussing culturally relevant communication. Teaching in the inner city meant that students used slang and AAVE (African American Vernacular English), and as their teacher I made that okay. Sometimes, I used it too. It did not mean either party was less intelligent; it allowed us to understand one another. In discussions about communication, I was clear to point out the differences between their home language (AAVE) and its "academic" equivalent. Ultimately the world around them does not communicate in a monolithic format. I wanted them to be able to be proud of their AVVE but also to be able to communicate effectively with others once they left my classroom, while at the same time understanding that their success in school also depended upon mastering Academic Language.

Students, much like your own children, mimic everything you say and do. Whether they're trying to make a joke or are naturally drawn to their teachers, they absorb certain habits and behaviors like a sponge to water. Learning that early on, I knew that if I let them teach me, they would let me teach them—just as if I was eager and willing, they would, in turn, be eager and willing. Not only do our students learn subject matter content, but they also learn how to perceive the world and people around them—first through communication then through interaction.

Think for a moment, how can you change the perspectives of your students if you don't first know what they are? Exactly, you can't. Culturally responsive educators will take time to learn their students' strengths, character, and habits; understanding students permits student-centered learning environments in which success can be the norm. Once teachers are able to determine how students think and function, they can make data-driven decisions about how those students can learn. Being culturally responsive is the key that unlocks a lot of barriers to success.

One thing teaching middle school will do is challenge you! I can think of several times where I tried teaching lessons in social science or history and the concepts just did not click until I revisited the strategy employed, changed it, and allowed the students to let me know what worked for them. Show me a challenge and I'll show you some champions. That's the mentality.

ECONOMICS CHAMPIONS

I recall teaching an economics lesson on supply and demand to my students back in 2017. One of the first questions they raised was, "Why are we doing math in social studies?" and in my mind, I'm like, "Right!? Why are we?" Rather than vocalizing this sentiment, I said in my best "teacher voice," "Because how people interact with the world around them is social" or something like that. I felt pretty confident as I flashed on my PowerPoint slides with cool graphs and other bells and whistles. But here's the part I missed: My lesson lacked cultural relevance. I was communicating to the students in a way that they couldn't connect to their past experience. I quickly realized that I had to pivot to something that they did understand and could relate to: supply and demand of Flaming Hot Cheeto sales. Not only did I allow them to take lead on the lesson, but I also gave "teacher privileges" to one of my students who would have normally been a behavior problem. He was a middle school entrepreneur, so he understood the game. My student being an educational resource added even more cultural relevance to the lesson because he could communicate with the students in ways that I could not—he was one of them. I watched from the back of my classroom in awe as he doodled on the whiteboard with his symbols and different markers, only relying on me for assistance with vocabulary. At first, it didn't make sense to learn about math in a social studies class, but the switch in strategy allowed the students to change their perspective and see how human or social activity was relevant to supply and demand.

POLITICAL CHAMPIONS

Taxation without representation. That mantra from our middle school years. While teaching about colonization and European exploration a challenging question came up from one of my students. She asked, "Why would they want to leave the king if he's providing them with everything they need? I mean they're from his country." Quite an interesting perspective she had. I used it as a teachable moment, and I let her know that she wasn't alone in that thought process. In fact, the people who thought like her were called Loyalists—a vocabulary word. Don't you just love when challenging moments allow your lessons to align?

I challenged that student and the entire class to think of the two countries involved like our homeroom classes; that was an easy concept to envision because the students kept up little homeroom rivalries with one another. I posed the question, "Would it be okay for Mrs. Apples to control what happens in my homeroom, especially if she has never been here? Why or why not?" That's when the murmurs started, and the students got territorial. Eventually, many of them began to understand the different effects of colonization and could sympathize with the patriots—another vocabulary word—as they would, too, have wanted autonomy in livelihood and decision-making absent of ridiculous taxes from overseas. Again, show me a challenge and I'll show you some champions.

If you want to get the best out of students, send someone who not only looks like them—meaning someone who understand their beliefs, motivations, and concepts they hold true. Teachers have to stop being the "No Pencil Police" and really learn from their students to get a holistic understanding of who is coming into their classroom and the best methods that can be used to facilitate an environment in which students can learn.

Students' understanding of school and education is built at home, but polished in the schoolhouse. The reality I faced teaching middle school students was that not all of my students desired to go to college, therefore their motivation and involvement and certain lessons and activities differed. Not everyone saw the purpose of learning about the Five Themes of Geography or Western Exploration. As their teacher, I was tasked with figuring out how to teach them beyond the motivational differences they had. You have to ask yourself, "How can I reach this scholar? What is important to them?" Once you are able to answer those types of questions, you become more culturally responsive, and you increase your chances of quality output from your students.

Working in my former school district, the vast majority of the students I taught and worked with lived below the poverty line and within a food desert. For those reasons alone, their motivation for getting up and going to school was different from others with different circumstances. I knew that every day couldn't be a great day no matter what the morning announcements said. Student A may not have been able to sleep through the night, so they napped in class. Student B made sure their little brother had a pencil for school, so they don't have one. Student C didn't eat dinner, so they want to snack on chips even though the classroom rules say otherwise. This is where the Pencil Police have to learn to "L.I.G. a Little" or "Let It Go a Little."

Instructional time can't be spent addressing the minors—we as educators have to focus on the majors. Are your students present? Are they prepared? Keep going! I'm not encouraging you to burn the rules—I'm encouraging you to become realistic. Ask yourself a few questions: Is this a major or a minor? What can I do differently that changes some outcomes? How can I support these students? What does reinforcement look like in my culturally responsive classroom? Can I redirect this behavior and still support the needs of my student(s)? Are they the problem or is it my perspective?

What I've learned during my time in the classroom is that students are responsive when they feel seen. Below you will find a list of strategies that you can use that allow students to feel seen and have some autonomy in their learning experiences.

1. **Be Yourself**

   Students can always tell when you are the true and authentic version of yourself. It is best that you learn their culture without appropriating it. Walking in your truth as an educator will set a positive example for students and foster a relationship of trust and authenticity. Over the years, I've taught a number of Spanish-speaking students. I took it upon myself to learn a few words so I could interact with them similarly to the way I interacted with other students. I would greet them in their maiden language and even allow them to teach me words. This made them feel comfortable and enjoy coming to my class, which in turn led to motivated students who produced great work and had positive attitudes.

2. **Student-Led Lessons**

   Peer-led instruction and activities are excellent ways to promote culturally relevant pedagogy. Students are able to communicate with one another in a way that some educators cannot, especially if there is a barrier like age or culture that gets the wires crossed. Together, students are able to use culturally responsive terms to communicate, which can promote positive interaction, fluent critical thinking, and overall content retention.

3. **Give Students Voice and Choice in Showing Their Knowledge**

   No matter what students appear to be on the outside, one classroom is typically bursting with diversity on the inside. It is imperative for educators to know and understand the learning preferences of their students and offer them a variety of ways to express themselves and demonstrate their knowledge; they tend to perform better when they are allowed to engage with content through methods and strategies, in which they excel. Consider real-world based prompts or project-based learning activities. Some students will excel at writing while others may want to speak or create a multimedia project. Allowing students to choose not only allows them some autonomy, but it promotes confidence and empowers students to integrate cultural elements in their planning and execution processes.

4. **Use Student Vocabulary**

   Key terms are oh so important, but they can also be confusing to someone who has never heard or seen the word. Oftentimes, the barrier to students understanding vocabulary is cultural—the word may not have ever been used in their household or in context by anyone they know. Additionally, vocabulary is sometimes *defined using other words that may incite some confusion. A great way to relinquish that barrier would be to use student vocabulary. Use words students are most familiar with coupled with content-specific terminology. That way, students are communicating comfortably and learning new words, and it lessens the chances of students experiencing discomfort about learning. The goal is to make sure they learn, not to overcomplicate the process.*

— Dr. Arianna Stokes

Dos and Don'ts

It can be hard for a student to understand or relate to someone who is far removed from their own life experiences. Oftentimes, we may teach students that are so unlike us that they shut down before we have even opened our mouths. That is when it is okay to look for assistance from others who look like your students, such as your colleagues, guest speakers, or mentors. But above all, put yourself in the role of a learner and *learn from them.* When you invest in furthering your understanding of your students' lived experiences, you will be in a better position to win their trust and break down differences.

DO:

- Understand your cultural differences and how they may or may not align with those of your students.

- Seek assistance from others on how to speak with and guide students who are not connecting with you.

- Offer a space for a natural connection to grow from your own cultural awareness.

DON'T:

- Think you automatically have what it takes to connect with a crowd of students who are nothing like you.

- Be naïve and try to relate to students by using slang or words that are unfamiliar to you; this can read as offensive.

- Try to lie to fit in; that won't be received well, and kids can see right through fakeness.

Chapter Reflection

Realizing that you don't know what you don't know may be humbling, but it can take you far. In this chapter we have received some great insight from a superb practitioner of culturally responsive pedagogy. Think back to what you've read in this chapter and determine how you can authentically connect with your students. And don't feel you have to go it alone. Colleagues and others from the students' own communities are there to help you.

Have you ever missed an opportunity to truly connect with a student because you did not want to seek help? If so, how could you have changed that with cultural responsiveness?

_____

_____

_____

_____

In what ways can you make time and space for people who look like your students to connect with them? Where in your lessons can you incorporate such exposure?

_____

_____

_____

_____

Being culturally responsive can make you look at yourself in a new light. Describe a time when your unintentional bias inhibited your pedagogical implementation.

_____

_____

_____

_____

CHAPTER 9

Dreams Lead to Education

Capture Their Passions in Your Lessons

Imagine an ideal classroom full of fun and art. Now imagine a class of musically gifted and ethnically diverse children who travel around the world in a rocket named Rocket that is controlled by artificial intelligence. These kids are talented and excited about learning new and fun things. They sing and play instruments, and, most importantly, they learn to be critical thinkers because their perspective on learning has no predetermined limit. If this sounds familiar, perhaps you have encountered Leo, Annie, Quincy, and June—the Little Einsteins. *Little Einsteins*, a public access television show for preschoolers, is full of adventures that introduce kids to nature, world cultures, and the arts. I have seen how the Einsteins' adventures activate a child's willingness to learn, and even as an adult I can remember parts of their catchy theme song. The show lit a passion for learning and curiosity in me because the world the Einsteins inhabited was dreamlike. But oftentimes students lose that passion for learning as they get older, and it takes more than the Little Einsteins to ignite their dreams.

When dealing with students who are disengaged, you must first know how to get their attention and maintain that attention for a long period of time. In the past, our response to such students was remediation—the "drill and kill" approach—which is the antithesis of what they actually need. Such traditional methodologies can fuel a negative perspective on school: Students feel school is forced on them, which undermines their sense of safety and hinders their capacity to learn. A healthy alternative to remediation is activation, or exciting students' imaginations and learning about their interests and passions. When you teach to students' passions, you are igniting their dreams and launching their rockets! Once students can envision how school will help them pursue their dreams, they will begin to take an interest in their classes and come to appreciate the benefit of formal education. Activating a student's passion is how you can begin to change that student's outlook on school—the subject matter of this chapter. Shifting perspectives in this manner can help stimulate your students' appreciation for school and also potentially change them in deeper ways.

← IGNITE THEIR DREAMS: ACTIVATE THEN EDUCATE

We can spend lots of time espousing the virtues of schooling as the pathway to fulfilling our students' dreams, but for even the most persuasive of educators, this won't always work for every student. When you run into such an impasse, try flipping the proposition: Dreams lead to education.

Steve Harvey (2019), a popular TV host and comedian, once said, "If you have a kid that wants to be an airplane pilot, you can quit talking to him about education; talk to him about being a pilot. If you ignite his dreams, he will do math and science. Once he starts dreaming, you got him." The use of such reverse psychology can be powerful indeed. Rather than beating the drum on education as the subject of the sentence, make it the object and lead with *dream*.

The best two things you can give kids are hope and vision. They have to wake up in the morning dreaming about something that connects them to a passion to persist. But when their day-to-day experience is disconnected from the dream, it's hard to sustain hope. In other words, when we overkill on school as being the answer to every student's problems, it becomes an unhelpful trope that only serves to widen the disconnect between the student and schooling.

The future belongs to those who believe in the beauty of their dreams. — **Eleanor Roosevelt**

Igniting a student's dream calls upon you to first ask some fundamental questions: What holds the student's attention? What is the student's essence? What motivates the student? What does the student want out of life? As we've seen, accessing a student's dream necessitates shutting up and listening. Once you are able to find the answers to these questions, you can then find ways to address the student's passions in your lessons.

My wife and I stressed out many nights trying to figure out ways to get my son excited about school; he was just not motivated. Like so many of our students he had formed a negative perspective on school. He would sometimes make comments like, "School isn't for me," or express how much he hated school. Just because my wife and I believed in the value of school did not mean that our son would automatically buy into *our* concept of school. For years he continued to do just enough to get by, which frustrated us because we knew how much potential he had. Before you form any preconceptions, I want to be clear that my son is an amazing kid that never got into any trouble. Everyone in school spoke highly of him—until it came to academics. He just wasn't driven by education. And, as his parents, we felt strongly that the root cause wasn't poverty or racism: To be blunt, unlike me, my son grew up privileged—he ate every day, had a house, didn't share a room, and always had clean clothes.

The only thing that got my son's attention was the thought of becoming a cop; he would stay up all night watching cop shows. He wanted to be a police officer to the point that he actually redecorated his room to resemble a police station. Ever since elementary school he had been able to break down police codes because of the time he spent researching the codes on the Internet.

Let's pause right here—did you catch that? He was studying on his own to do something that had his attention. You don't have to convince kids to do what they already want to do; as a matter of fact, you can't always *stop* a kid from doing something when they really want to do it!

Kids and adults both somehow make the time for what they want to do. So for years all my son studied was the behavior of cops—how they walk, how they talk— he even took on the posture of cops. Any time he would see one, he would go crazy with joy. Whenever we were riding and he saw a police car go by, he would turn around in his seat and stare at the passing car with fascination. That's a teachable moment. Now imagine if he had made a connection with a teacher who had taken the time to understand his likes and who activated his passion even more by making lessons relatable. A teacher who had used the police codes to help him see the importance in math and context clues. A teacher who had used a suspect's description to teach him about descriptive language in literature. A teacher who had integrated forensic science into biology lessons. With a bit of effort and a spark of creativity, it can be done! Take a small amount of time to learn about your students' interests and apply your creativity to address them in your lessons. It can work wonders!

ACTIVATION

I remember a pastor asking me how to get our kids to come to church in their community. My response was, "Enlist the aid of someone who looks like your kids, or, in a broader sense, someone who speaks your kids' language. Someone who can speak to their dreams, or just someone who is able to relate to them." You may recall these prerequisites from the previous chapter. I went on to explain that the pastor might not have the ability to reach these children in the way that others might. That's a lesson for us all, and that's okay—that's why we need help from the community. So, after years of failing to motivate my son to put effort into school, I knew I needed to get creative. I had to enlist the aid of someone who spoke my kid's language. I met a police officer who was really cool, so I asked him to talk to my son. He was someone who had influence and who was able to tap into my son's dream of being a cop. This officer explained the role of law enforcement to my son and even let my son accompany him on a ride-along. He explained that there was more to being a police officer than what meets the eye. He was able to activate my son's dream and allow him to make the connection to education. With a child who seems unreachable, begin with activation. More often than not, the education spark will naturally follow.

IT'S THEIR DREAM, NOT YOURS

My wife and I wanted to support our son's policing dream, but we had our own perspective on the best route to realizing it. We knew that he would need to attend the police academy, but we wanted him to complete college first and pursue a major in criminal justice. The more we pushed, the more he began to hate the idea of attending college. We realized that we had more to gain by allowing him to engage with police officers who were willing to expose him to their daily lifestyle and who could motivate him in ways that we couldn't.

Our son made it clear that if he went to college, he was destined to fail because he didn't like school. Once again, I had the clarity of vision to realize that I had to back off and better understand his perspective.

So again we shifted to supporting him and his dreams instead of pushing our expectations. We increased his exposure to anything related to policing, and eventually he came across a job as a dispatcher for the local police department. He loved this idea so much he filled the application out himself and went alone to get his background check and fingerprints. He was determined to get that job! He began to ask us for help with all manner of things related to the job—a sharp contrast to the days in which we couldn't even convince him to bring home a form from school that required our signatures. (This happened even when the teacher offered 100 points for his daily grade simply if he returned the signed form. He would forget it in his bag or not even care to give it to us.) This may sound extreme, but I know that nearly every educator has encountered students like my son.

> *To be a human being is to be in a state of tension between your appetites and your dreams, and the social realities around you and your obligations to your fellow man.* — **John Updike**

When my son wanted something, he did what was needed to get it. When he got the job, he had to do a few weeks of training that required him to be at work by 6:00 a.m., and he would be dressed and out of the house by 5:00 a.m., all on his own with no help from us, which was so atypical considering our years of struggle to wake him up for school every morning. Moreover, he now came home after each day of training talking excitedly about what he had learned. He even participated in a volunteer training program for several weeks, which extended his days even longer. My son was barely getting sleep because he was consumed by training and other matters related to his certifications.

Now he is dreaming in his own space at his own pace. He's a man who lives in his passion. Not long ago he told me, "I have a new goal. I want to become a detective. I'll be going to college for criminal justice." I broke down inside as I thought back to our struggle to persuade him to attend college. I now realize that my wife and I had to first broaden our own perspectives from belaboring what our son *should* do (think back to Chapter 2) to instead appealing to his dream. I believe there is an important lesson here for educators: Persistence matters! You may not get it right the first time, but if you take the time to access your students' passions, they will find their own way to realizing their dreams.

 DEBIT CARD ACTIVATION

When you get a debit card in the mail, the first thing you have to do is what? Activate that card. No matter how much money you have in your account, you can't use the card until you activate it. Consider how this metaphor might apply to your students: No matter how much potential they have, it won't be realized until it is activated. Just as you have to pull that strip back and activate that debit card, you must peel back the layers of your students before they can start using their potential.

My sixth-grade teacher would tell me every morning that I was amazing. Believe it or not, some students have never heard that adjective used to describe them before. My teacher knew she had to build my esteem before I would gain the confidence to succeed. She also made me come to the board to solve math problems while telling the other students, "Watch Tommie get it all right." My mind might be telling me, "No, I'm not," but my teacher knew exactly what she was doing. Every time I went home, I'd make the effort to complete every assignment she doled out because *I couldn't let her down.* She set the bar high for me, so I refused to make her look bad, especially after I knew she was there to support *me* and she was *for me.*

When students know they can trust you and you have their best interests at heart, those students will fight for you. They just want to feel that they matter. Educators also matter! Never walk into that building feeling like you are insignificant no matter what your role is in your school. Every moment you spend with a child is a teachable moment.

ACTIVATE THAT PASSION

As a student I had a classmate who never came to school. And I mean, *never.* But he was a really good artist. He would paint amazing, lifelike portraits as well as some of the most wonderful street art. Street art is widely misunderstood; some still associate it with thugs and vandals, but it takes considerable talent to make a portrait come to life on the side of a boxcar or the back of a building.

On one of those rare days when my artist peer showed up in the building, one of his teachers stopped him in the hall. This teacher, whose subject was art, said, "I'm glad to see you here, and I want to see some of your artwork." This blew my friend's mind. Instead of the art teacher chastising him, he was uplifting him without even knowing it.

So my friend showed up the next day with some of his canvases. And that one day led to his coming to school every day. And he came only for art! He developed a relationship with that art teacher, and the teacher made an agreement with him one day by saying, "I tell you what, come to all your classes and at least score Cs, and I'll buy you art supplies each payday." This was an offer my friend could not refuse. He not only came to school and improved his grades but he went on to go to college and graduated with a liberal arts degree in art. He is now an extremely popular photographer. He is so successful that he has a list of clients booked for months in advance and has had to hire an assistant for his studio. That's activating a dream!

Think about the connection that art teacher made. He was able to activate his student's passion in a way that allowed him to ignite his dream and ultimately become a successful artist. That's meeting a child where they are; that's an effective pedagogy.

Dos and Don'ts

Students don't always see what we want them to see. Sometimes they only see the *right now*, and in the *right now*, they don't see how $y=mx+b$ is going to put money in their pocket or how it is relevant to their lifestyle. Remember that when creating a safe space for students to learn and grow.

DO:

- Find what interests students and build on that interest.
- Design lessons that help you get to know your student's dreams and desires and plan subsequent lessons that connect to those dreams.
- Ignite a passion within the student and then worry about educating them.
- Allow students to see how their education can work with their passion by exposing them to new ideas within their field of interest.

DON'T:

- Belittle students for their dreams, making those dreams seem unimportant to their education.
- Force facts on a student to just enable them to pass a test.
- Make a student think that college is the only way to be happy or make a living.

Chapter Reflection

In this chapter we have explored how the dreams and lifestyles that our students crave can motivate them to perform. Kids might not want to do something, but they will do it if they understand that putting in the effort will allow them to pass that course to get them one step closer to their dream. Have you noticed that most athletes only perform well during their sport seasons? Why is that? Because of eligibility: They are willing to do just enough to be eligible for the season. Having been a college athlete, I can tell you that if it wasn't for my sport, I wouldn't even have been in college. I've known other college athletes who have said the same. The lesson here is that we shouldn't try to deny our students their interests and passions. Instead, we just need to address those interests in creative ways to help shape their perspective. Use the spaces below to help you reflect on how you can ignite dreams.

Why, as an adult, is a dream important to you? How can you take that knowledge and build a connection with your students?

How can you begin to understand your students' dreams? List activities you can try in your next classroom to help make this happen.

Think of a time when you could have planned an enrichment activity for your students. How could you have used such an opportunity to ignite your students' passions?

CHAPTER 10

What Shaped My Perspective?

Your Students Need You

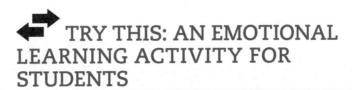 TRY THIS: AN EMOTIONAL LEARNING ACTIVITY FOR STUDENTS

Think about your various perspectives and how they shape you and your world. Next, engage your students in a similar process. Have your students describe their perspectives on education on a piece of paper and also document the emotions that rise up as they articulate those perspectives. The act of making these perspectives visible and recognizing their accompanying emotions not only provides you, the educator, with important insights but it also enlightens your students.

A common outcome of this activity is that some students articulate their fear and discomfort around schooling. When offered the opportunity to express these anxieties, this can alleviate some of the burden they carry—an initial step toward shifting perspectives. A continuous theme of this book is that a student's perspective can determine that student's success or failure in school and in life. In my experience, the students who have the most difficulty coping with their emotions are the most apt to fear school. But remember that self-knowledge is power! A simple statement like "School isn't for me" can have many layers beneath the surface. As you work with students to unpack these layers, you'll find that you are in a better position to assist them, and, at the same time, they will be in a better position to help themselves.

➡ WHAT SHAPED MY PERSPECTIVE?

I am the youngest of six children. I have a sister and four brothers. Life was tough growing up with five older siblings, but I was able to wreak havoc on them and essentially escape the punishment because I was the youngest. The large age difference made it hard to connect with them. I was always viewed as a burden placed upon them by my parents while they worked or slept, or as a pest when I just wanted to hang out with them. I can hardly recall any moments from my childhood in which I felt like I was a welcome sight to my siblings.

They were very good at communicating how much of a burden I was to them. None of them seemed to understand my lack of happiness because they were blinded by *their* unhappiness. I don't believe I was deliberately being neglected, but to a small child, it certainly seemed that way. My logic was convoluted, but it made perfect sense at the time: If I was unhappy, others should be unhappy too. I acted on this belief in destructive ways. I began cutting the wires to my brothers' television and game consoles. I destroyed my sister's dolls and physically attacked her friends when they came over. I believed that if the things that made them happy were taken away, then we could all be unhappy together. At the very least, we could spend time with each other. Of course, that didn't happen.

Early on I developed low self-esteem—the outcome of my belief that no one wanted to be around me. My parents loved each other, but they argued frequently. I remember crying with my sister outside their door when we heard them fighting with one another. My dad didn't fit the profile of an abusive husband. In retrospect, I realize that he was hurt and angry that Mom was cheating on him. Mom would come home at all hours of the night, and once she arrived the arguing began.

However, to outsiders, we seemed to be a happy family because we were together. My mom went to bingo every other night. Sometimes I tagged along, as did my siblings. At times we stayed so long that we fell asleep on top of the bingo tables. We often stayed until the place closed. Sometimes when my mom went to bingo, she took the money needed to pay the household bills, which inevitably led to more fights with my dad, some of which ended with trips to jail for domestic violence. It would hurt and anger me so much when my parents fought. My mom started making trips to the hospital for stress-related illnesses. She was on the verge of having a mental breakdown.

Let's pause. Try to digest what I've disclosed so far. Now think about your students. Like I did, your students may also be enduring barriers beyond their control that hinder their learning process. Cultivating an awareness of such barriers (and students' lived experiences in general) is essential to understanding how to overcome them. My story encompasses several common components of childhood adversity, such as neglect and domestic violence. This double whammy led to trauma that no doubt affected my learning outcomes and behavior.

By the time I was six, I had absorbed the name I had heard for so long—*troublemaker*. While attending first grade, I became a teacher's worst nightmare. I fought daily and stole students' lunch money. I played tricks on my teachers just so I could make the kids laugh—things like putting glue in their desks. I mastered being a menace.

By second grade I had been suspended at least twelve times. It was so bad that a teacher told my father that if I were to return the next year, she wouldn't teach anymore. I knew that every time I got into trouble, my father would be called. Although he would be upset, I cherished the time spent being lectured by him. During those lectures he asked questions and seemed interested in what was going on with me. I was eventually kicked out of that elementary school and placed into a program that was geared toward troubled youth. I was then kicked out of that program, too.

Before reaching my teen years, I was forced to deal with a lot of responsibility. My dad worked overnight, and it was up to me and my sister to keep the house in order. She would cook and clean and try to be a mother to me. But my sister and I both ran the streets at night because no one was there to tell us not to. Words cannot express how much I missed my mom.

By the fourth grade, I had been kicked out of three schools. Things were getting worse, yet I kept outdoing myself. By fifth grade I had already attended seven schools, and my behavior was not improving. I was also arrested during my fifth-grade year for breaking and entering. I went on to get expelled from three middle schools and had to repeat eighth grade. By then I had been kicked out of ten schools.

In those years I looked up to the guys that were getting acceptance and what seemed like respect from other people. I wanted that same thing. I was drawn to guys with gold teeth in their mouths and tattoos. Why? Because these were the cultural artifacts of my community. Also, both my mother and father had golds in their mouths and tattoos. I picked up on these influences and began to accumulate ink and permanent gold teeth by middle school—just like my parents. (I later had the gold teeth surgically removed during my senior year in college.) My intent is not to suggest that forms of expression such as tattoos are a deficit. They simply represented a different form of cultural expression that didn't fit the norms of the schools and only served to further typecast me as a menace.

At this point I need to say that it was never a personal dream that made me pursue education. I loved sports and was an athlete. I knew that if I didn't get the grades, I wouldn't be eligible to play sports, so I did what I could to just get by. But when the season ended, I would go back to failing and skipping classes. I didn't really start caring about school until I started playing Amateur Athletic Union (AAU) basketball. I had coaches who took me on the road with them and exposed me to how the top players in the country approached life.

I credit AAU for saving my life. When I was on the road and staying in hotels with these guys, I met other ballplayers from other states that were dreaming big. They told me they wanted to go to North Carolina and play for Duke University. My realization ("Y'all dream differently than me") caused some dissonance, but then I started to think *I could do it, too.* I could go to college someday and play basketball.

In my senior year of high school, while I was skipping school, I was accidentally shot in the foot.

I did eventually make it to college, but not for a while. My mindset ("Maybe I *am* smart enough") and attitude ("Maybe I *should* be in school") had begun to shift. However, think back to the perspective pyramid diagram at the beginning of the book: Modifying these two variables alone is not sufficient to change a person fully. Without a full shift in perspective—the lens through which you see the world and make meaning of it—it's hard to undo lifelong patterns.

Perspective influences thoughts, which shapes attitudes, which produces results.

Going from being labeled an "at-risk" student to becoming a teacher in the same school district that expelled me ten times to now being a very successful educational consultant has given me the experience to understand and communicate from the perspective of both student and teacher. As a former teacher in an urban school district, I applied many of the principles described in this book to my hard-to-reach students. As a teacher working with many students who had endured adverse childhood experiences (a concept that is unpacked later in this chapter), I had to tap into specific tools that my infuencers had used to shift my perspective towards education. For example, I still think back to my sixth-grade teacher (mentioned earlier in the book) who not only helped elevate my self-esteem but who fully understood what it meant to a teacher.

I certainly suffered my share of hardship, but there was one silver lining in my childhood: I began to develop a close relationship with my neighbor—the girl of my dreams. She provided everything I had craved in a friend and a sibling. We were so close that our parents joked about planning our wedding. Time seemed to fly when I was with her. Unfortunately, tragedy struck when she was taken from me by a drunk driver. I remember this awful moment like it was yesterday, and even now the memory still reduces me to tears.

I will never forget the frantic phone call from my sister, who was crying hysterically. She informed me that my friend had been rushed to the hospital after having been struck while riding a go-cart with her friend. The driver had ignored a stop sign and plowed into them. I couldn't think clearly, but I knew I had to find my way to hospital to see her.

By the time my dad and I made it to the hospital, her family and friends were gathered in the waiting room. I ran to the back to see her and passed her mom on the floor, sobbing. I held my friend and told her it was going to be fine. In the moment I believed she would bounce back and we would be talking on the phone again soon. Then her mom, who had risen from the floor, told me she had died instantly. Then it was me who collapsed to the ground.

Nothing in the world could have ever prepared me for that loss. I couldn't stop weeping. My mind and spirit were so overwhelmed with grief that I didn't want to talk to anyone for a long time. I didn't want to get close to another person ever again. I just couldn't endure such agony again.

Let's take another pause to digest my story. One of the saddest truths in life is that bad things can happen to innocent people, including our kids. Adverse childhood experiences (ACEs) occur regularly to children ages zero to eighteen years across all races, economic classes, and geographic regions. ACEs are most prevalent among those children living in poverty. ACEs include emotional abuse, physical abuse, sexual abuse, emotional neglect, physical neglect, mother treated violently, household substance abuse, household mental illness, parental separation or divorce, and incarceration of a family member (Centers for Disease Control and Prevention 2021).One study determined that children exposed to four or more ACEs are thirty-three times more likely to have a learning or behavior problem compared to children without ACE exposure (Burke et al. 2011).

Extensive research on ACEs and their effect on academic achievement has been conducted over many decades (see, for example, Hunt et al. 2017). Once I became more knowledgeable about ACEs, I realized that I had already endured four or more of them before I even made it to my teenage years. Without even knowing it, I had already been set up to fail.

Do you think this was enough to shift my perspective on life? I am a living example of how one's deeply rooted perspective can shift and alter one's life circumstances. I have come full-circle and now have a completely different outlook on life and school. In my case it took tragic circumstances to ultimately change my perspective, but thankfully this isn't always a prerequisite. Sometimes it just takes a great mentor or teacher who has the ability to spark something in you that leads you to change your perspective. My greatest hope is that my readers will learn from my story and strive to understand their students' perspectives as well as their own. Providing some hope and helping to change the life of one child will always be worth it, but always remember that as an educator you have the power to save *many* lives.

Everybody thinks you should be happy just because you're young.
They don't see the wars that we fight every single day.

The above quote was taken from another one of my favorite movies, *Freedom Writers*. In this 2007 film, a dedicated teacher in a racially divided Los Angeles school has a class of at-risk teenagers deemed incapable of learning. Instead of giving up, she inspires her students to take an interest in their education and plan their futures. She assigns reading material that relates to their lives and encourages them to keep journals. Initially her students do not take well to the idea of sharing their stories with someone who seems to be a stranger. Why? Because just like I did as a child, they feel that they will only burden their teacher, and, moreover, they don't think anyone will care. But the perseverance of that one teacher in learning what influences shaped her students was all it took. She kept pushing herself to know them.

Think about an opportunity now where you can make a connection. Your students need it. Your students need *you*. Very few people were able to reach me when I was young. Now is the time for me to pay it forward. I was saved by God's grace, and teachers have that ability to be a graceful presence to students who really need them.

As I conclude, I am now *Dr.* Tommie Mabry, and, while I don't claim to know everything, I can state with certainty that educators really do matter! Regardless of your role in your school, never walk into that building feeling that you are insignificant. Anytime you are around a child is a teachable moment.

References

Avildsen, J. G. (1989). *Lean on me*. Warner Bros.

Bandura, A. (1977). *Social learning theory*. Prentice-Hall.

Burke, N. J., Hellman, J. L., Scott, B. G., Weems, C. F., & Carrion, V. G. (2011). The impact of adverse childhood experiences on an urban pediatric population. *Child Abuse & Neglect, 35*(6), 408–413.

Byrne, R. (2006). *The secret*. Simon & Schuster.

Centers for Disease Control and Prevention. (2021). *Preventing adverse childhood experiences*. Retrieved October 14, 2021, from https://www.cdc.gov/violenceprevention/aces/fastfact.html

Children's Defense Fund. (2020). *The state of American's children 2020: Child poverty*. Retrieved October 8, 2020, from https://www.childrensdefense.org/policy/resources/soac-2020-child-poverty/

Coburn, R. (2020). Principles not rules: Living & learning in the real world. *Life Learning Magazine*. Retrieved October 4, 2021, from https://www.life.ca/lifelearning/0512/Principles_Not_Rules.htm

Cooper, A. R., Page, A. S., Wheeler, B. W., Hillsdon, M., Griew, P., & Jago, R. (2010). Patterns of GPS measured time outdoors after school and objective physical activity in English children: The PEACH Project. *International Journal of Behavioral Nutrition and Physical Activity*. Retrieved October 14, 2021, from https://ijbnpa.biomedcentral.com/articles/10.1186/1479-5868-7-31

Copeland, K., Khoury, J., & Kalkwarf, H. (2016). Child care center characteristics associated with preschoolers' physical activity. *American Journal of Preventive Medicine, 50*(4), 470–479.

Delale-O'Connor, L., Alvarez, A., Murray, I., & Milner, H. R. (2017). Self-efficacy beliefs, classroom management and the cradle to prison pipeline. *Theory into Practice, 56*(2), 178–186.

Duhamel, F., & Talbot, L. R. (2004). A constructivist evaluation of family systems nursing interventions with families experiencing cardiovascular and cerebrovascular illness. *Journal of Family Nursing, 10*, 12–32.

Dweck, C. (2007). *Mindset: The new psychology of success*. Ballantine.

Fiore, N. (2014). The benefits of movement in schools. *The Creativity Post*. Retrieved October 4, 2021, from https://www.creativitypost.com/article/the_benefits_of_movement_in_schools

Freire, P. (1972). *Pedagogy of the oppressed*. Herder and Herder.

Gay, G. (2018). *Culturally responsive teaching: Theory, research, and practice, third edition*. Teachers College Press.

Hammond, Z. (2015). *Culturally responsive teaching and the brain: Promoting authentic engagement and rigor among culturally and linguistically diverse students*. Corwin.

Harvey, S. (2019). *Motivated*. Facebook Watch. Retrieved October 14, 2021, from https://m.facebook.com/SteveHarvey/videos/dreams-more-important-than-education/450663102256545/

Heick, T. (n.d.). *What did Paolo Freire believe about education?* Teachthought.com. Retrieved October 7, 2021, from https://www.teachthought.com/education/an-excerpt-from-pedagogy-of-the-oppressed-by-paulo-freire/

History.com. (2009). *Marcus Garvey*. Retrieved October 8, 2021, from https://www.history.com/topics/black-history/marcus-garvey

Hunt, T. K. A., Slack, K. S., & Berger, L. M. (2017). Adverse childhood experiences and behavioral problems in middle childhood. *Child Abuse and Neglect, 67*, 391–402.

Jalongo, M. R. (2005). Editorial: On behalf of children. *Early Childhood Education Journal, 32*(5), 281–282.

Jongsma, J. (2018). *Ellen DeGeneres surprises New Jersey principal with $50,000 donation from Cheerios.* Northjersey .com. Retrieved October 4, 2021, from https://www.northjersey.com/story/news/essex/2018/09/14/ellen-dege-neres-surprises-new-jersey-princi-pal-50-000-donation/1308784002/

Kaufman, P., & Owings, J. (1992). *Characteristics of at-risk students in NELS:88.* National Center for Educational Statistics. Retrieved October 7, 2021, from https://nces.ed.gov/pubs92/92042.pdf

LaGravenese, R. (2007). *Freedom writers.* Paramount Pictures.

Learning-theories.com. (2020). *Social learning theory (Bandura).* Retrieved October 7, 2021, from https://www.learning-theo-ries.com/social-learning-theory-ban-dura.html

Little Einsteins. (2009). Distributed by Walt Disney Studios Home Entertainment.

Macmillan, F. (2018). *Learning styles: Kinaesthetic learner characteristics* [Editorial]. Engage-education. Retrieved October 14, 2020, from https://engage-educa-tion.com/

Mansfield, F. (1991). Supervised role play in the teaching of the process of consultation. *Medical Education, 25,* 485–490.

Maslow, A. H. (1943). A theory of human motivation. *Psychological Review, 50*(4), 430–437.

May, C. (2018). The problem with "learning styles." *Scientific American.* Retrieved October 12, 2021, from https://www .scientificamerican.com/article/the-problem-with-learning-styles/

McNaughton, D., Hamlin, D., McCarthy, J., Head-Reeves, D., & Schreiner, M. (2007). Learning to listen: Teaching an active listening strategy to preservice education professionals. *Topics in Early Childhood Special Education, 27*(4), 223–231.

Neumann, D. A. (2016). *Kinesiology of the musculoskeletal system* (3rd ed.). Mosby.

Olivares-Cuhat, O. (2011). Learner factors in a high-poverty urban middle school. *Perspectives on Urban Education, 9*(1), n.p.

Robison, T. (2020). Improving classroom management issues by building connections with families: Part 1. *General Music Today, 33*(3), 36–39.

Rosenthal, R., & Jacobson, L. (1968). Pygmalion in the classroom. *The Urban Review, 3*(1), 16–20.

Safin, S., & Dugan, J. (2021). *Street data: A next-generation model for equity, pedagogy, and school transformation.* Corwin.

Saphier, J. (2017). *High expectations teaching: How we persuade students to believe and act on "smart is something you can get."* Corwin, Learning Forward, PDK.

Schaedig, D. (2020). *Self-fulfilling prophecy and the Pygmalion effect.* Simply Psychology. Retrieved October 8, 2021, from https://www.simplypsychology.org/self-fulfill-ing-prophecy.html

Major, S. (2016). *Teaching strategies that meet the needs of kinesthetic learners.* Child1st Publications, LLC. Retrieved October 12, 2021, from https://child1st.com/blogs/resources/113159303-teaching-strat-egies-that-meet-the-needs-of-kines-thetic-learners

Texas Education Agency. (2016). *Measures of student growth.* TEA Student Growth Overview. Retrieved from https://www .childrensdefense.org/policy/resources/soac-2020-child-poverty/

Van Leeuwen, D. (2000). *Marcus Garvey and the Universal Negro Improvement Association.* National Humanities Center. Retrieved October 8, 2021, from http://nationalhumanitiescenter.org/tserve/twenty/tkeyinfo/garvey.htm

Vygotsky, L. S. (1978). *Mind in society: The development of higher psychological processes.* Harvard University Press.

Index

ACEs (Adverse childhood experiences), 31, 55, 90–91
active listening, 10–11, 13, 15–16
Adverse childhood experiences. *See* ACEs
assessments, 40–42
at-risk students, 38, 89
attention, student's, 64, 78
attitudes, 1, 4–6, 29, 89

beliefs, 1, 3–6, 21, 23, 29, 68, 70, 73, 87
biases, 14–15, 26, 28–30, 38
body language, 14–15
bus stop, 46

changing a child's perspective, 2
childhood, 53–54, 71, 87, 90
Children's Healthcare, 8
child's perspective, 3, 30–31, 63
cohort, 27, 65–66
colleague, 8–10, 12–13, 28–29, 54, 69
college, 29–30, 48, 70, 73, 80–81, 83–84, 89
color, 5, 31, 40, 51
community, 4, 26, 28–29, 51–52, 70, 76, 80, 89
connection, 9, 11–14, 16, 18, 24, 29, 32, 70, 79–80, 83–84, 92
conversation, 2, 10–11, 14–15, 17, 27–28, 56, 62, 70
creativity, 23, 41, 79–80
curriculum, 27, 61–62, 68

data, satellite, 39–40
Dos and Don'ts, 15, 23–24, 33, 41, 49, 57–58, 66, 75, 83
dreams, 77–78, 80–81, 83–84, 90

effort, 1, 3–6, 14, 29, 36, 48, 79–80, 82, 84
emotions, 5, 86
expectations, 19–21, 24, 37, 68, 80

fight, 17–18, 20, 53–56, 82, 87, 91
fit, 19, 55, 58–60, 75, 87, 89

Freire, 27, 29–30
friend, 7, 17, 22, 47–48, 82–83, 90

high school, finished, 30, 32
high school dropouts, 31, 38

interviews, 63–64, 69

Kaneesha, 56
kinesiology, 60, 62
kinesthetic learning, 60–62, 64–65

library, 47–48
listening, 7–11, 14, 22, 78

Marcus, 47–48
marginalized students, 24, 40, 45, 61–62
Maslow, 45, 57
medical students, 11
middle school, 8–9, 61, 71, 88–89
mindset, 4–6, 23, 89
motivation, 32, 45–47, 50, 70, 73
movement, 60–64, 66

options, 17, 32, 49–51, 64–65

passions, 32–33, 67, 70, 77–79, 81–85
patients, 11–12, 70
pedagogy, responsive, 68, 70, 76
perspective
   shifting, 78, 86
   survival, 25
   unique, 20
perspective shifts, 5, 32
police officer, 79–80
positive perspective, 1, 3, 40–41, 65
principles, 14, 17, 21–23, 58, 60, 64–65, 90

rules, 8, 20–23, 38, 54, 73

school community, 5, 63
school failure, 38

shift, 4–5, 13, 24, 32–33, 89–91
shoulds, 19–21
space, safe, 57–59, 83
standardized tests, 39–40
stories, 7, 10, 18, 26–27, 46–47, 53, 88,
    90–91
student-centered learning environments, 71

student growth, 35, 40–41

teaching middle school
    students, 73
trust, 11–12, 51–58, 65, 74–75, 82

values, 3–7, 10, 32, 41, 52–53, 70

A SAGE Publishing Company

Helping educators make the greatest impact

CORWIN HAS ONE MISSION: to enhance education through intentional professional learning.

We build long-term relationships with our authors, educators, clients, and associations who partner with us to develop and continuously improve the best evidence-based practices that establish and support lifelong learning.

Solutions
YOU WANT

Experts
YOU TRUST

Results
YOU NEED

INSTITUTES

Corwin Institutes provide regional and virtual events where educators collaborate with peers and learn from industry experts. Prepare to be recharged and motivated!

corwin.com/institutes

ON-SITE PROFESSIONAL LEARNING

Corwin on-site PD is delivered through high-energy keynotes, practical workshops, and custom coaching services designed to support knowledge development and implementation.

www.corwin.com/pd

VIRTUAL PROFESSIONAL LEARNING

Our virtual PD combines live expert facilitation with the flexibility of anytime, anywhere professional learning. See the power of intentionally designed virtual PD.

www.corwin.com/virtualworkshops

CORWIN ONLINE

Online learning designed to engage, inform, challenge, and inspire. Our courses offer practical, classroom-focused instruction that will meet your continuing education needs and enhance your practice.

www.corwinonline.com

PLSN209A8

Visit **www.corwin.com**

CORWIN